Relevance of Thempu in Pastoral Ministry

Relevance of Thempu in Pastoral Ministry

A Socio-Theological Perspective

Paul Lelen Haokip

Bethesda Khankho Institute

&

Christian World Imprints

First Published in 2020 by

Bethesda Khankho Institute
Centre for Integrated Studies
Churachandpur-795128
bkiindia2020@gmail.com
Phone: +91 9665580993

&

Christian World Imprints
Christian Publishing & Books from India
C-3, Wazirpur Industrial Area
Delhi-110052
cwidelhi2017@gmail.com
www.ChristianWorldImprints.com
Phone: +91 11 41526079

ISBN: 978-93-5148-457-8 (HB)
ISBN: 978-93-5148-458-5 (PB)

Cover photo taken by Rev. Dr. Lamboi.

Printed in India.

DEDICATION

This scientific research is dedicated to all the indigenous *Thempus* of *Kuki* history who have contributed their wisdom and skills for the welfare of the society. May their loyalty and attitude of service continue to inspire readers of this literary piece.

I also dedicate this work to all those persons who have shared me their knowledge about indigenous *Kuki Thempu* tradition during my research schedule. May wisdom and knowledge worthy of preservation continue to flow from generation to generation.

Contents

Foreword

The book, 'Relevance of Thempu in Pastoral Ministry' is a ground-breaking project as the author ventures into exploring the richness and relevance of indigenous wisdom for pastoral ministry which never was a possibility until a recent past. The form of Christianity that came to indigenous Kuki people in the latter part of the 19th and early 20th centuries did not give a room for indigenous expression of faith and practice. They were viewed only to be discarded in the process of 'civilization.'

With a strong conviction that the ancient practices of the indigenous Kuki *Thempu* could enrich vice-versa the understanding and practice of pastoral ministry, the author formulated three broad guiding questions to carry out his research. He asks - what exactly was the role of *Thempu* in Kuki indigenous tradition, What is the relevance of *Thempu* for the contemporary society and how would *Thempu* enhance pastoral ministry particularly within Catholic priesthood.

The strength of the book lies in the followings. First, it is the outcome of firsthand empirical studies which included observations, discussions and interviews with elderly local experts as well as knowledgeable indigenous scholars in the field across all denominations and traditions in Kuki society. For this reason, it is a pioneering work in this particular field.

Second, the author unearthed the then major role *Thempu* played in the lives of the villagers. The scale of his contribution is reflected in his in-depth study of *Thempu* and what it involved to be a *Thempu* in indigenous Kuki culture. He rightly pointed out that the eligibility of a *Thempu* was not confined to his intellectual knowledge and skills but also his lifestyle of integrity and approachability to all. *Thempu* was a mediator between the human world and the spirit world. It was a life of complete surrender and dedication for the task of public service being equipped with both knowledge and spiritual power. The role of *Thempu*, in that sense, was more than a profession as the author succinctly explained.

Third, having provided an academically well-grounded understanding of the role of *Thempu*, the author then attempted to connect *Thempu* with Catholic priesthood. In this connection, the researcher proposes that indigenous *Thempu* tradition and Catholic priesthood can enhance each other by collaborating traditional and biblical practices. His main argument is that revisiting one's cultural roots, for instance, *Thempu* tradition, relishing those rich cultural heritages and integrating them with Catholic priesthood could make the liturgy more relevant to contemporary people. A Catholic priest and an indigenous *Thempu* are committed to God and people. Their normal day-to-day works circle around people for spiritual or material need. They first owe allegiance to God and then to their personal interests. The author further observes that both *Thempu* and Catholic priesthood have the God-given power to bring grace and blessings upon people. The author convincingly argues saying that in all ways, both *Thempu* and a Catholic priest are communitarian people, set apart for religious acts, and serve as source of inspiration for others.

The book is an excellent resource for those who are interested in interdisciplinary studies in general and students of indigenous studies, contextual theologies, pastoral ministry, ethnography, ethnohistory and cross-cultural mission.

As an indirect and timely contribution, the book also paves the way for convergent movement among the people towards unity in faith articulation and expression. The indigenous *Thempu* tradition is a common and unifying practice among all Kuki tribes. By leading the people back to their common tradition, the author brings the people together for faith expression and action. This book must find a place in the book shelves of committed pastors, ethnographers, indigenous leaders and sustainable community advocates.

Rev. Dr. Jangkholam Haokip
Director, Bethesda Khankho Institute
Centre for Integrated Studies
Manipur, India

Acknowledgement

At the completion of this project, I sincerely thank God for bestowing me good health and many resourceful persons to guide me. It has been a fruitful in-depth journey to the past, finding meaning and evolving relevance from indigenous wisdom.

I would like to thank Most Rev. Dominic Lumon, D. D., Archbishop of Imphal, Manipur. His constant motivation and focused guidance were a directional inspiration. My sincere gratitude to MISSIO for co-sponsoring my research on *Thempu*.

I express my profound gratitude to Dr. (Fr.) Konrad Noronha S.J., for his insightful supervision in the field of qualitative research and helped me polish my raw data into a presentable literary piece. His guidance has given me a direction to explore the nuances of the indigenous *Kuki Thempu* tradition and its relevance in the present Catholic priesthood practice.

I owe my sincere gratitude to many respondees whom I have interviewed during my research phase. Their acumens and detailed descriptions of the then indigenous *Kuki* priesthood – *Thempu* - has given me a chance to relate and evaluate its relevance from a socio-theological perspective within the Catholic priesthood tradition.

Enormous assistance of the library of Jnana-Deepa Vidyapeeth, Pune, India, enabled me to discover the depth of Catholic Priesthood. I sincerely owe my gratitude to the library workforce. Sincere words of thankfulness to my MPM classmates, friends, and well-wishers for their constant encouragement and support. They have been my refuge and source of inspiration.

The original title was "Relevance of Thempu in Catholic Priesthood: A Socio-Theological Perspective for Effective Pastoral Ministry." This has been modified for pastoral reasons. It is now titled as "Relevance of Thempu in Pastoral Ministry: A Socio-Theological Perspective."

I owe my sincere gratitude to Rev. Dr Jangkholam Haokip, Director, Bethesda Khankho Institute, Churachandpur, Manipur, India. Thank you for your sustained support and scholarly interventions to this piece of work. I am inspired by your constant innovations to integrate indigenous wisdom in different streams of your undertakings. Thank you Bethesda Khankho Institute for publishing this project. May those who read this literary piece be inspired to enhance the *Thempu* tradition.

Paul Lelen Haokip
paulhowkeep@yahoo.co.in
paullelenhaokip@gmail.com
https://paullelenhaokip.blogspot.com/

Onomasticon

Thadou	:	One of the names of indigenous *Kuki* ancestors
Thadou-Kuki	:	Following a ruling of the Guwahati High Court, the Government of Manipur issued an Order dated 12/05/1987 to the effect that the name of the dialect/ language shall henceforth be known as 'Thadou-Kuki' for the purpose of literature or Major Indian Language (MIL) subject until further orders. Retrieved from e-pao.net › news section › Press Release › Press Release 2016
Thempu	:	The indigenous *Kuki* priest
Pathen	:	Holy Father, God
Vaiju	:	Wine made from fermented rice with husk (local beer)
Chung Pathen	:	Heavenly God
Pooyas	:	Sacred writings of the *Meiteis* in Manipur
Cheitharol Khumbaba	:	Royal Chronicles of the *Meitei* Kings in Manipur
Del	:	Cloth worn by *Kuki* men to cover the waist and below
Tuhsombem	:	Rounded up hair pitched on the upper part of the head

Mangvom	:	A *Kuki* traditional shawl with black fringes on either side
Manmasinao	:	Sons and daughters of Manasseh
Thilha	:	Spirit of something, someone's spirit
Changkhatpu	:	A lone man of a family
Chollaivom	:	A spot in human eyeball that blinds them from seeing spirits
Si thing	:	Oak tree
Indoi/Doibom	:	Basket that holds indigenous *Kuki* cultic materials of worship, a household God or symbol of household worship object, household spirit
Gopi	:	The King of bamboos
Khaopi	:	The King of robes
Kelchal kiheh	:	Curved horn of a he-goat
Vohpi maikem	:	Curved skull of a mother pig
Mimpi	:	Job's tears, cereal normally grown by indigenous *Kukis*
Changpi	:	Rice
Lhalho/Kilhalho	:	Ritual for blessing of the soul of a person
Lhakou	:	Calling of the spirit of a person in times of sickness or loss
Chang-Ai	:	A festival of feeding an entire village after the woman of a family harvests great amount of paddy
Sa-Ai	:	A festival of feeding an entire village after a man has killed a great number of big and dangerous animals
Chon	:	Festival to commemorate the climax of *Chang-Ai* or *Sa-Ai* or *Gal-Ai* to show one's hard work, goodness, courage, success
Khopi Kilhaina	:	Ritual for the welfare of a village
Phunsan	:	A ritual of divination as to what would come in the future
Sanglai Tun	:	Bamboo basket chair where a dead person was seated

Hun	:	A time of festival during spring; a time for changing thc *Doibom*
Gamlahlang	:	Sickness or omen thought to have originated from forests
Kholailang	:	Sickness or omen that has its origin from village or people
Kin	:	Custom
Khopi Kilhaina	:	Worship, ritual, sacrifice for the wellbeing of a village
Kholhim	:	A ritual to hypnotize a village
Chang Lhakou	:	A ritual for inviting paddy's spirit
Sa Lhakou	:	A ritual for inviting an animal's spirit
Kilhakouna	:	A ritual for the soul of a person
Them sa	:	The upper portion of flesh on the spine, meat meant for the *Thempu*
Kaoshe	:	Evil spirit
Semang-Pachong	:	Cabinet members and auxiliary of *Inpi*
Inpi	:	Assembly
Haosa	:	The Chief, King of the village
Mithi Kho	:	Village of the dead
Lhanpelkot	:	Gate of the dead
Thijonbung	:	Mountain range of the dead
Sa-o	:	Necklace made of cotton thread and chicken feather for healing sicknesses
Sacerdotal	:	Priestly, relating to priests or priesthood
CBCI	:	Catholics Bishops' Conference of India
Them ju	:	A portion of wine offered to *Thempu*
Achegu	:	An upper portion of an animal killed at a ritual ceremony that is given to the priest as *Them sa*
Tuimit san	:	Divination with the albumen/glair of an egg
Cam	:	Free space made with bamboos or round wood in an indigenous *Kuki* house near the kitchen where wastes can be easily disposed
Vaiphit	:	The ritual of sprinkling *vaiju*

Chavang Kut	: An autumn post rice harvest festival of indigenous *Kukis*
Changlhah	: The *Kuki* traditional unleavened bread wrapped with banana leaves
Saipikhup	: The *Kuki* traditional shawl worn by men
Pucha	: A basket to measure paddy or use for storing something
Kithoina	: Ritual for healing
Kangui	: A wild rope used during rituals of sick people
Ai	: A wild turmeric used in rituals
Sel	: Mithun, Bos Frontalis (Shaw, 1979, p. 22), gayal, a price animal in the *Kuki* society, used for marriages, feasts and rituals
Dah	: Gong
Maimom	: An insect used for the ritual of *Lhakou*
Pumpeng	: Hollow reed for keeping *Maimom*
Godal	: A open basket used for cleaning rice
Sanglai Tun	: Dead person seated in a basket in the middle of the house
Kep	: A wooden post erected on the grave to show valour or hunting skills
Akilha	: Traditional farewell for a woman from her family members
Khulsamnu	: The evil spirit that harasses the departed souls of non-achievers of *Sa-Ai* or *Chang-Ai* on their way to the abode of the dead
Nangjang	: Slit bamboo used for tying things
Galngam and Hangsai	: Indigenous *Kuki* mythical persons thought to be experts in magic
Lumen Gentium	: (22 November 1964) Dogmatic Constitution on the Church, solemnly promulgated by His Holiness Pope Paul VI
Gaudium Et Spes	: (7 December 1965) Pastoral Constitution on the Church in the Modern World,

		promulgated by His Holiness, Pope Paul VI
Sacrosanctum Concilium	:	(4 December 1963), Constitution on the Sacred Liturgy, by His Holiness Pope Paul VI
Optatam Totius	:	(28 October 1965), Decree on Priestly Training, proclaimed by His Holiness Pope Paul VI
Presbyterorum Ordinis	:	(7 December 1965), Decree on the Ministry and Life of Priests, by His Holiness Pope Paul VI
Humanae Vitae	:	(25 July 1968) Encyclical Letter of the Supreme Pontiff Paul VI to His venerable Brothers, the Patriarchs, Archbishops, Bishops and other Local Ordinaries in Peace and Communion with the Apostolic See, to the Clergy and Faithful of the whole Catholic world, and to all Men of Good Will, on the Regulation of Birth
Familiaris Consortio	:	(22 November 1981) Apostolic Exhortation of Pope John Paul II to the Episcopate, to the Clergy and to the Faithful of the whole Catholic Church on the Role of the Christian Family in the Modern World
Mystici Corporis Christi	:	(29 June 1984) Encyclical on the Mystical Body of Christ, to our Venerable Brethren, Patriarchs, Primates, Archbishops, Bishops, and other Local Ordinaries enjoying Peace and Communion with the Apostolic See, by Pope Pius XII.
Donum Vitae	:	(22 February 1987) The Instruction on Respect for Human Life in its Origin and on the Dignity of Procreation by

the Congregation for the Doctrine of the Faith

Pastores Dabo Vobis : (15 March 1992) Post-Synodal Apostolic Exhortation to the Bishops, Clergy and Faithful on the Formation of Priests in the circumstances of the present day, by Pope John Paul II

Evangelium Vitae : (25 March 1995) To the Bishops, Priests and Deacons, Men and Women Religious, Lay Faithful and all People of Good Will on the Value and Inviolability of Human Life, by Pope John Paul II

Vita Consecreta : (May 25 1996) Apostolic Exhortation of the Holy Father John Paul II to the Bishops and Clergy, Religious Orders and Congregations, Societies of Apostolic Life, Secular Institutes and all the Faithful on the Consecrated Life and its Mission in the Church and in the World

Laudato Si : (24 May 2015) Encyclical Letter of the Holy Father Francis on Care for Our Common Home

Semantics : The branch of linguistics and logic concerned with meaning

AIACHE : All India Association for Christian Higher Education

Leitmotiv/Leitmotif : A recurrent theme throughout a musical or literary composition, associated with a particular person, idea, or situation

Gen : Genesis

Ex : Exodus

Num : Numbers

Deut : Deuteronomy

Ps : Psalms

Wis : Wisdom

Matt : Matthew

Mk	:	Mark
Lk	:	Luke
Jn	:	John
Act	:	Acts of the Apostles
Rom	:	Romans
I Cor	:	I Corinthians
2 Cor	:	2 Corinthians
Phil	:	Philippines
Heb	:	Hebrews
Gal	:	Galatians
Col	:	Colossians
1 Pet	:	1 Peter
1 Jn	:	1 John

General Introduction

At the outset, I delimit my research work amongst *Thadou-Kuki* dialect speaking group of *Kukis* in Manipur, India. There could be other historical *Kuki* tribes who have similar values, myths, and culture, of which I am not confident to refer to. Therefore, I shall deal with what I know for clarity and authenticity. While hailing from the North East of India, ironically, I am having in-depth research of my culture after sufficiently influenced by western Christianity. My humble attempt is to situate indigenous *Kuki Thempu* culture within Christianity and bring more relevance in Catholic liturgy. Though Christianity originated in the East, the indigenous *Kukis* have received westernized Christianity in the latter part of the nineteenth century. An element of estrangement developed with the arrival of Christianity as if the then thought-to-be-good indigenous *Kuki Thempu* culture has become impure and demonic all of a sudden. There is a displacement of the indigenous *Kuki* self within his or her own culture.

Christianity has been influenced by various cultural milieux at a given time and place. If we can speak of westernized Christianity and Roman Catholicism, can we also attempt to evolve a Tribal Christianity or indigenous *Kuki* Christianity without compromising Christ's values? As a researcher in ethnography and ethnohistory, I set out with no prior thesis, but open for assimilation and readiness to imbibe the indigenous *Kuki Thempu* culture within the larger *Kuki* cultural practices in the real-life environment with an endeavour to encapsulate *Thempu* culture.

The dissertation deals with the indigenous *Kuki* world view of spirits, God, *Thempu* and their relevance in pastoral ministry in general and Catholic priesthood in particular. With the progress of time, indigenous *Kuki* wisdom is fading away from the minds of its present community members. Accepting the fact that all the indigenous *Kuki* practices are not sacrosanct, the researcher finds that there are many indigenous practices worthy of preservation and continuation. These are immortal value-laden practices that meant a lot to the then indigenous *Kukis* and can still echo relevance even when viewed from the socio-theological lens of the Catholic priesthood tradition that exists in the Catholic Church today. The dynamics of learning from the past for the present realities become a much-needed tool for effective pastoring.

The first chapter introduces some primal beliefs that affect any indigenous tribal group. The themes of priesthood in general and Catholic priesthood in particular, are presented with the associated works expected of a priest. In the present *Kuki* society, indigenous respect accorded to nature is slipping away and cultural practices of indigenous *Thempu,* considered almost abhorrent with the arrival of western Christianity. Using scientific ethnographic research methodology, the researcher presents some relevant questionnaire to arrive at indigenous *Thempu* tradition that was primarily oriented to service and sacrifice.

In the pages of the second chapter, you will meet the indigenous *Kukis* in their sociological, historical and cultural perspectives with the influential position of *Thempu* in their day-to-day life. The indigenous *Kuki* belief in *Indoi/Doibom* in which God was represented by the finest elements in nature known to them will be discussed in detail. The village administration headed by the *Haosa*, the institution of marriage and concept of life beyond death is deliberated as found in the indigenous *Kuki* culture. The oral tradition has been judiciously handed down from generation to generation.

The third chapter offers a confluence of cultic rituals with Catholic rituals at the time of birth and baptism. The priestly services like administration of Sacraments, education and pastoral care for sick are underlined. The celebration of feasts in indigenous *Kuki* tradition is presented parallel with the celebration of Saints'

Day in the Catholic tradition. The chapter closes with the theme of *Thempu* and Catholic priests as intercessors for people.

The fourth chapter is a mine of face-to-face interviews with various knowledgeable persons in the field of indigenous *Kuki Thempu* tradition and other cultural practices. The world of spirits and human being's constant strive for a peaceful existence with spirits are discussed in comprehensive manner. The need for God's blessings at every movement of indigenous *Kukis* is the bedrock in this chapter. The chapter opens a new world of beliefs, festivals, and treatment accorded to dead people. The relentless struggle with evil spirits and desire to be near the good God is a theme that is existent in Catholicism as well.

The fifth chapter concludes with discussion for Pastoral Ministry and portrays the indigenous *Kuki Thempu* tradition involved in safeguarding human life and ecology. The motif of forgiveness, the respect accorded to women, sense of thanksgiving are areas for rich socio-theological reflection. Love of neighbour and wish for the wellbeing of others, care for ecosystem were treasured values in the pre-Christian indigenous *Kuki* culture which are Christian values upheld in entirety. In-depth research of indigenous *Kuki Thempu* tradition has shown values that congruently exists in the spirituality of Catholic priesthood.

Data were collected using personal in-depth interviews with people who were versed in the *Thempu* tradition. Sources of the research are from both Catholics, non-Catholics, written books and oral traditions of those who practised indigenous *Thempu* itself and from those who have seen or known about the *Thempu* tradition. Their contributions remain as infinite wealth.

In all-purpose, one can conclude that the indigenous *Thempu* tradition was for the holistic welfare of people in the village set-up governance. Care for the sick and constant war against sickness and forces of the evil encouraged much of the indigenous *Thempu* cultic practices. The mystic priestly rituals and care for the sick is a relevant leitmotif in the Catholic tradition too. Therefore, this research is an attempt to situate oneself in indigenous *Kuki Thempu* culture to unearth the nuances for relevance.

Chapter 1

Kuki Belief System, *Thempu* and the Catholic Priesthood

Introduction

Belief in some form of God had been present in the indigenous culture of *Kukis* even before they accepted Christianity. More than concepts, the indigenous *Kuki* people used symbols and signs to express and impress their relationships with Gods and one another. These indigenous ways of expression can hardly be accentuated in western languages nor the impregnated worldviews with implications in their given culture be translated satisfactorily. A symbol could conceal or disclose something. God has always been considered as the originator of humans and the earth itself. The indigenous *Kuki* worldview is necessarily a religious one that links man, nature and history directly to the only Almighty God called "Chung Pathen" (Changsan, 1992. p. 99) who is the creator, sustainer and sovereign God over all things, things in heaven and things on earth, visible and invisible, including powers and gods, and over all human beings. The indigenous *Kukis* attribute all kinds of goodness to *Chung Pathen*. God was also thought to possess feminity and masculinity. In rituals, God was addressed as

"Pathennu, Pathenpa" (Haokip, 2000, p. 20) which means "Mother God, Father God." To them, God was full of goodness, kindness, mercy, love, meekness and endurance. They believed that this good God does not interfere in the daily affairs of human beings nor demand sacrifices from people.

The indigenous *Kukis* also believed in benevolent spirits who aid while malicious spirits disturb the lives of village people. The daily lives of *Kukis* were rather occupied with appeasing evil spirits that trouble them at different occasions of life. The village priest's primary duty was to appease or ward off these evil spirits. He had additional work as a village doctor – to heal sicknesses and diseases that affected people of the village. The coming of Christian missionaries into indigenous *Kuki* land during the latter part of the 19th century, made the *Kukis* forsake their traditional religion and way of life. Hence, it has become difficult to authentically know the traditional religious life of the *Kukis* (Changsan, 1992).

Therefore, this research attempts to spot the then major role *Thempu* played in the lives of the villagers and establish a link of significance with today's Catholic priesthood. The relatedness of indigenous *Thempu* and Catholic priesthood, the mysterious nature of God and the occurrence of sickness could be the underlying bonds of interest. The indigenous *Kuki Thempu's* responsibilities can find its meaning in the Catholic priesthood existent today. They are more complementary than dichotomic.

1.1. Primal Instinctive Beliefs of the *Kukis*

Indigenous beliefs in spirits are not just an invention but a necessity for survival. Tribal worldview accords space to spirits in the cosmos. The belief in malevolent spirits roaming around human habitat or vice versa is not illogical. "Every culture in the history of humankind has included belief in the numinous as a major part of its understanding of reality" (Barnes, 2000, p. 29). The indigenous *Kukis* of Manipur are no exception to this belief.

Inquiry about primeval beliefs helps to recognize indigenous *Kukis*. "Primitive thought is woven into the greater complexities of later cultural forms, including ours. Primitive religions still live in the niches of contemporary culture and in the corners of our personalities" (Barnes, 2000, p. 12). Various indigenous *Kuki* beliefs are filled with mystery and mysterious rituals which when explained in a language foreign to that particular culture are at times inadequately expressed. Chryssides (2014) states, "Religious activity is not self-explanatory, especially if a ritual is conducted in a language" unknown to researchers or students. In this scenario "Rahner's notion of infinite mystery as the ultimate context of human life" (Barnes, 2000, p. vii) becomes relevantly active and meaningful. The primary purpose of religion is to enable its followers to have closer contact with a Supreme Being and to "answer life's fundamental questions, not to provide data for researchers" (Chryssides, 2014, p. 68). The sense of mystery increases to an outsider while an insider may relish the mystery per se. Ignacimuthu (2010) has rightly pointed out, "The tribal people are sensitive to spirit-presence in the world around them. In many tribal societies, the Divine is often seen as a pervasive, diffuse spirit-presence throughout the Cosmos, the Earth, and natural phenomena" (p. 44). In the indigenous *Kuki* society, everything in nature was considered having a soul.

Ethnographers frequently define their role as "making the strange familiar and the familiar strange" (Chryssides, 2014, p. 67). Knowing about indigenous *Kuki* society opens up a world of surprises and at the same time induces a mysterious world of beliefs. In *Gaudete Et Exsultate*, in his Apostolic Exhortation on the Call to Holiness, Francis (2018) points out, "God infinitely transcends us; he is full of surprises. We are not the ones to determine when and how we will encounter him; the exact times and places of that encounter are not up to us" (no. 41). God can be encountered in people, places, cultures, situations, etc.

At times, primal rituals are termed as magic by outsiders. Magic is "infrarational while that of religions is supra-rational" (Bouyer, 1999, p. 13), assuming human beings' radical dependence on powers superior to them. According to indigenous *Kuki* belief, spirit or God was supposed to be present everywhere in nature. Therefore, each ritual performed becomes an encounter with powers superior to them. In rituals, man (a person) encounters powers surpassing himself with words, rituals or gestures (Bouyer, 1999). A sense of mystery surrounds the ordinary life of indigenous *Kukis* in their agrarian cycle of life from choosing a field, slashing trees, plantation, harvest and ingathering of crops, festivals, birth, sickness, death, and life after death. The belief in malevolent spirits disrupting human habitat was a persistent menace for the indigenous *Kukis* society.

1.2. Cultural Evolution

No culture can be rigidly stagnated. With the passage of time and existential experience, modifications do creep in. Another word for culture may be 'tradition' that is passed on or handed over to someone. Religion and rituals have normally been at the heart of every tradition. The basic beliefs, values, and practices are part of the cultural air each person breathes that become part of life (Barnes, 2000). There is a cultural evolution.

Indigenous *Kuki* culture has undergone tremendous evolution with the arrival of Christianity. As religion powerfully "influences culture, culture also conditions religion" (Barnes, 2000, p. 190). In the indigenous *Kukis* culture of usual feasts, customary practices and rituals where *vaiju* was used have been replaced with ordinary tea along with customary acts of agreement. Undeniably, every culture and society is formed over many generations influenced by historical experiences – sociologically, economically, religiously. Every culture is "human inventiveness at work, over thousands of years, discovering endless possibilities of languages, law, custom, value, roles, rules, all the things that go into making us who we are" (Barnes, 2000, p. 190). Custom thus evolves and dissolves with time. The office of *Thempu* was one such central custom amongst the indigenous *Kukis*.

1.3. Priesthood in General

There are numerous forms of the priesthood in various indigenous communities around the world. Indigenous *Kuki Thempu* tradition is one such kind. Ambrose C. Agu (2009) succinctly describes the general priesthood thus:

> A priest is generally understood as a ritual expert of a religious group, who, possessing the knowledge of the techniques of worship, leads the group in offering sacrifices, praises, and adoration to the Supreme Spirit. He is a sacred

> person in his group and is often regarded as its religious functionary responsible for the valid execution of ritual acts in accordance with the demand of the supernatural beings associated with the group. (p. 67)

Priests are leaders to enable the meeting between people with God. Paul VI (1965), in *Optatam Totius,* Decree on Priestly Training exhorted care for "especially the poor, the children, the sick, the sinners and the unbelievers" (no. 8). Christ's caring spirit is inculcated in Catholic priests from the initial stage of formation period. In many but varied ways, indigenous *Thempu* was associated with care for the sick in his particular village – almost the jurisdiction of his priestly ministry, which is akin to a Catholic parish priest's area of ministry. In *Lumen Gentium*, Paul VI (1964) wrote:

> The ministerial priest, by the sacred power he enjoys, teaches and rules the priestly people; acting in the person of Christ, he makes present the Eucharistic sacrifice and offers it to God in the name of all the people. But the faithful, in virtue of their royal priesthood, join in the offering of the Eucharist. They likewise exercise that priesthood in receiving the sacraments, in prayer and thanksgiving, in the witness of a holy life, and by self-denial and active charity. (no. 10)

Therefore, every person can be considered a priest by participation and witness of Jesus Christ's life and ministry.

1.4. Formation to the Catholic Priesthood

The vocation to indigenous *Thempu* is comparable to Catholic priesthood extending to long years of discernment until voluntary commitment to serve God and people. "During these initial years, the candidates are accompanied by one or more community members who offer the wisdom, guidance, explanations and needed information, and encourage personal growth and community involvement" (Serrao, 2010, p. viii). In the case of indigenous *Thempu* tradition, there were older *Thempus* who would guide the aspiring young *Thempus*. Whereas, in the Catholic Church, the task of the formator is to help the candidate discern the authenticity of a religious vocation, to pay attention to God's personal communication (Serrao, 2010). Paul VI (1965), in *Optatam Totius*, stresses the importance of formation, stating:

> Pastoral concern which ought to permeate thoroughly the entire training of the students also demands that they be diligently instructed in those matters which are particularly linked to the sacred ministry, especially in catechesis and preaching, in liturgical worship and the administration of the sacraments, in works of charity, in assisting the erring and the unbelieving, and in the other pastoral functions. (no. 19)

The formation to Catholic priesthood is long and tough with chances for personal reflection before sacerdotal ordination.

1.4.1. Voluntary Vocation

When freedom of choice is curtailed, there is slavery in place. Free and purposeful choice make the chooser responsible and oriented. "Open-ended reflection and choice" (Barnes, 2000, p. vii) make a decision self-binding and value-laden. Induced decision to accept the vocation of indigenous *Thempu* or Catholic Priesthood implies the absence of a free will. To be a *Thempu* in the indigenous *Kuki* tradition and to be a Catholic priest are vocations purely free of individual choice after serious personal and communitarian reflection. Pope John Paul II (1992), in *Pastores Dabo Vobis* beautifully accentuates the value of freedom thus, "This gift of God does not cancel human freedom; instead, it gives rise to freedom, develops freedom and demands freedom" (no. 2). The community has the power to appreciate or object the candidate to priesthood based on authentic behavioural patterns. "In the choice of vocation, there is a process of psychological exploration of oneself, of the context of life and of history" (Serrao, 2010, p. 61) conforming to particular norms of the Catholic tradition. The ongoing self-formation and exploration of the inner self to discern whether one is truly and freely willing to adopt the vocation of indigenous *Thempu* or Catholic Priesthood need profound reflection. To make a free choice, personal maturity is necessary. This choice once made, should not be stagnated or definitive but rather undergoes a process of continuous maturity enhancement. Perhaps, it "could be refined and perhaps redefined throughout the whole course of formation" (Sarrao, 2010, p. 62) and during involvement in pastoral ministry. Thus, in the true sense, a vocation to priesthood remains an ongoing formation. Paul VI (1965) stressed in *Optatam Totius*, "Teachers and all those who are in any way in charge of the training of boys and young men, especially Catholic associations, should carefully guide the young people entrusted to them so that these will recognize and freely accept a divine vocation" (no. 2) for the service of people. The community of entrusted lay leaders also play a vital role in the formation to priesthood. The family, local society, the church members contribute to the formation of priests overtly and inertly. It becomes a communitarian endeavour.

1.4.2. Person of Communion

The Catholic priest is instructed on "history, structure, theology, divine grace, and spirituality" (Rossetti, 2004, p. 117). He needs to do all these to build an authentic communion with people. In Post-Synodal Apostolic Exhortation, *Pastores Dabo Vobis*, John Paul II (1992) suggests to prudently "contextualize the subjects of priests, viewing it in terms of today's society and today's Church in preparation for the third millennium" (no. 5). This formation would aim towards the formation of priests to develop a healthy relationship with people. The very lifeline of the Catholic Church is being universal in communion with diverse groups around the world in a "harmonious tension between them" (Rossetti, 2004, p. 117). The underlying motive is that "the priesthood envisions principally the apostolic life, principally for others" (Hoffman, 2001, p. 47). The priest should further initiate communion between spirits (God) and people or between people themselves. In the words of John Paul II (1992) in *Pastores Dabo Vobis*, the priesthood is "radically communitarian," and that "of special importance is the capacity (of the priest) to relate to others" (no. 49). A priest is to be a "man of communion" (Rossetti, 2004, p. 120). The priest has to learn to work with different groups of people with dissimilar views and calibre. John Paul II (1992) continues to stress in *Pastores Dabo Vobis*, "The whole formation imparted to candidates for the priesthood aims at preparing them to enter into communion with the charity of Christ the good shepherd" (no. 57). Formation aims to present Christ to humanity in specific contexts of ministry. The priest must become a living witness of Jesus who "went about doing good" (Acts 10:38).

In the Old Testament, God chose Israel as a nation proclaiming to them "For all the earth is mine, but you will be for me a kingdom of priests and a holy nation" (Ex 19:6), you will be called "priests of the Lord," you will be named "ministers of our God." In addition to that privileged choice, the patriarch, as heads of families or tribal groups, performed priestly functions such as offering sacrifices. We have incidents of Abraham trying to offer his only son Isaac (Gen 22:1-14), Jacob offered a sacrifice of a treaty (Gen 31:43-54). "You are a chosen race, a community of royal priesthood, a holy nation, a people God has made his own to proclaim his wonders" (1 Pet 2:9). The primary function of a priest is to initiate and enhance communion between God and people.

1.4.3. Colonial Imperialism on the ***Kukis***

The experience of being colonized in one's land is a painful experience to an insider but perhaps just a piece of historical twist for an outsider. In the book, Zale'n-Gam: The Kuki Nation, Haokip (1998) describes the crumbling of *Kuki* homeland into bits and pieces:

> The Kukis, having embittered the British particularly during 1917-1919 and 1942-1945, realized that there was no hope for them under the British rule. In order to permanently cripple the Kuki nation, the British divided the Kuki inhabited land (Zale'n-gam) into two, giving half to Burma and the other half to India. Thus, independent Burma saw the Kukis being scattered in two countries viz. Burma and India, and subsequently into three countries with the creation of east Pakistan/Bangladesh. (p. 20)

This artificial international boundary created by the British empire has caused immense socio-economic, political and cultural fragmentation in the lives of *Kukis* to their disadvantage. Colonial imperialism may refer to "that the superior cultures of Europe ought to dominate lesser cultures" (Barnes, 2000, p. vi). While the indigenous *Kuki* practices were the things known to them, the then arrival of western Christianity consistently insisted that Christian culture was superior to anything. This repetitive agenda diminished indigenous ethos. Traditional faith gave way to Christ-centred faith. Barnes (2000) tersely narrated western superiority thought pattern over others, stating:

> Individual religious traditions have proposed that the reason for belief lies in the actions of the divine power. Western religions, for example, have claimed that they believe in God because this God related himself to them. But, these same believers do not think the Zeus really appeared to the Greeks, or nature spirits to primitives. (p. 30)

Indigenous *Kukis* have found spirits and their belief in spirits profoundly embedded in their culture and semantics. The superior attitude of western belief to be true and indigenous beliefs to be less-true does not serve as an acceptable platform for dialogue. Christianity that was brought to *Kukis* in later part of the 19th century came with the same colonial imperialistic air of dominance.

The colonial British not only colonized indigenous *Kuki* land but also imperialized their culture largely. However, the freedom-loving indigenous *Kukis* did not sacrifice their physical freedom when asked to join the Labour Corps in France. "The Kukis were left with no option but to prepare for the defence of their sovereignty, against the insatiable colonial thirsts for territorial expansion. This resistance is termed as 'The Kuki Rebellion 1917-1919'" (Haokip, 2008, p. 141). While political insecurity existed on one side, the indigenous *Kuki* society was struggling with human sicknesses that could only be treated by their *Thempus*.

1.5. Research Problem Statement

The olden understanding and significance of *Thempu* in the indigenous *Kuki* culture are gradually diminishing from the minds of the younger generation. The onset of Christianity has also added to its non-significance. Therefore, what is called for is to rejuvenate the prominence of indigenous *Thempu* tradition as of pre-Christian era and find its significance in the Catholic priesthood.

There have been independent studies on traditional *Kuki* religion or *Kuki* tradition and culture. However, there has never been an attempt made by any person at "Relevance of *Thempu* in Pastoral Ministry." This is an ethnographic study that looks at indigenous *Thempu* tradition within the *Kuki* culture in the light of Catholic priesthood.

1.6. Research Questions

The following broad questions are formulated to gather authentic information regarding indigenous *Thempu* tradition within the *Kuki* culture. What is the role of the *Thempu*? What is the significance of *Thempu* in today's world? What *Thempu* traditions could be integrated into Catholic Priesthood?

1.7. Significance of the Research

The vast majority of indigenous *Kukis* who belong to various denominational churches could begin to have a better understanding of the significance of Catholic priesthood. Strictly speaking, protestant churches do not have the office of the ministerial priesthood, but many religious leaders are slowly addressing themselves or allowing others to address them as *Thempu*. It is intriguing to know that indigenous *Thempu* and his works were vehemently condemned and now the same people are taking the name *Thempu*. On the whole, Catholic priests, deacons, catechists, denominational church leaders, pastors, evangelists, etc., can critically ponder on various requirements and responsibilities of being a relevant *Thempu* in the present scenario. This research will contribute to a proper understanding and significance of indigenous *Thempu* in the light of Catholic priesthood at a deeper level, primarily attuned to service. This research will also find indigenous culture - a common ground for a spirit of ecumenism among the indigenous *Kuki* Christians.

1.8. Research Design

The researcher has employed a Qualitative Research method trying to elicit first-hand information through personal interviews at nine different locations within the Archdiocese of Imphal, Manipur, India. The research is an ethnographic study of the understanding of priesthood, indigenous *Kuki Thempu* as understood by Catholics and non-Catholics–men and women. Reeves (2008) views that ethnography is the study of social interactions, behaviours, and perceptions that occur within groups, teams, organizations, and communities. Added to that, Kuper (2008) gives strong emphasis on exploring the nature of a particular social phenomenon, rather than setting out to test hypotheses about it. Therefore, the research is to situate understanding of indigenous *Kuki Thempus* rather than to expect them to be where one wishes.

1.8.1. Participants

The participants were persons of 50 years and above. They were people who either practised, still practising, have reliable knowledge about indigenous *Thempu* tradition. They were cooperative, ready to share their knowledge and happy that their indigenous knowledge would be in written form someday.

1.8.2. Questionnaire (Appendixes A & B)

There are nine broad questions with four sub-questions, designed to elicit practices and nuances of indigenous *Thempu* tradition. One example of the open-ended question is - Describe people's or your understanding of *Thempu*. For those who did not follow English, the translation into *Thadou-Kuki* dialect would be like *Thempu chungchanghi mipite hetdan le nangma hetdan neihil in.*

1.8.3. Data Collection Method

The researcher used face-to-face interviews of 12 different persons lasting 60-90 minutes. The data were collected within 60 days. Information was collected from nine different locations consisting of five districts (Imphal, Chandel, Tengnoupal, Churachandpur and Kangpokpi) of Manipur, India.

1.8.3.1. Setting

The face-to-face interviews were conducted by the researcher in person, within the State of Manipur, India, during the months of

April and May 2018. The questionnaire was spoken to interviewees in *Thadou-Kuki* dialect and their consent voluntarily invoked. For those who could read English, the "Consent Form" was given to them and their due signature obtained voluntarily. The reason and significance of the research were amply made known to all interviewees.

1.8.3.2. Selection and Sampling

The interviewees were carefully selected comprising of six Catholics and six non-Catholics, and a woman participant. They were persons who practised indigenous *Thempu* tradition or had a fair knowledge of the indigenous practice. The transcripts were coded to deidentify the participants (example, JTH, GKZ, etc). Then, data were analyzed using themes.

1.9. Data Analysis Description

The qualitative research methodology is employed to elicit data and its subsequent analysis as well. The raw data collected have been put into themes for better comprehension and relevance that could initiate an effective implementation of experiences for Pastoral Ministry.

Conclusion

Every culture has its gradual development that could extend to thousands of years. Before the advent of Christianity among the indigenous *Kukis* of Manipur, India, the *Thempu* tradition was upheld for various socio-theological reasons in relations to sickness and appeasement of spirits. Dupuis & Neuner (2011) highlights how Pope John Paul II concludes the necessity to understand humanity's development, thus:

> Humanity has before it two modes of development. The first involves culture, scientific research and technology, that is to say, whatever falls within the horizontal aspect of the human being and creation which is growing at an impressive rate... The second mode of development involves what is deepest in the human being when transcending the world

> and transcending self, the human person turns to the One who is the Creator of all. It is only this vertical direction which can give full meaning to people's being and action, because it situates them in relation to their origin and end. (p. 185)

Indigenous *Thempu* tradition and Catholic Priesthood ultimately depend on God the Creator for survival and solace. The source of these offices springs from the mysterious nature of God. While their prime office of being a ritual expert remains intact, there is a need to imbibe wisdom from culture, science, nature, technology, sociology and theology. They remain channels of communication between God and people. Sickness, an element of the influence of evil spirit is a challenge to conquer.

The next chapter deals with the indigenous *Kuki* worldview, its various institutions for village self-governance and means for survival. The concept of God and his ever-abiding presence in the form of *Indoi* (household God) is elaborated.

Chapter 2

Understanding Indigenous *Kuki* Culture

Introduction

The uniqueness found in a particular culture is what distinguishes itself from others. Haokip (2008) states, "Culture may be stated to represent human life portraying human achievements; shared learned behaviour that refers to a group or community's way of life and outlook of the world, their values, norms followed and the material goods they create" (p. 71). The author continues to point out, "Elements of culture that commonly feature in ethnological literature are language, customs, beliefs, values, artefacts, symbols, religious practices, rituals, material traits, mythology, art, marriage and inheritance" (p. 71).

Many tribes around the world worship in their given ecological state of affair. Beliefs and religions have arisen from constant interactions between people and their surroundings. The life of tribals is usually connected to nature and symbols. So also, is the lifestyle of indigenous *Kukis* in Manipur who are attached to nature and derive meanings in symbols connected to nature. The belief in the presence of spirits in almost everything is strongly seen in the worldview of the indigenous *Kukis*. Chongloi (2008) states that "*Kuki* religiosity can be said condensed in the institution of *Indoi*" which may be translated as "House God" (p. 5). They believe that *Pathen* (God) has created spirits for the trees, stones, animals and other creatures. The *Thempu* was a connecting factor to consult, appease and remind the people about the anger of the spirits, mind of the spirits and of *Pathen* (God). He constantly sought the intervention of the omnipresent God who created the universe. Schmidt-Leukel (2017) claims, "Religions have imparted meaning and purposefulness, and despite all their dark aspects have contributed to the best and highest achievements of human life" (p. 20). The indigenous *Kuki* cultural practices, rituals, myths are what makes them unique from other ethnic groups.

2.1. *Kukis*

According to Col Reid (1893), the term "Kuki" is a Bengali word meaning "hill-men" or "highlanders" (Haokip, 2008, p. 2). The *Kukis* love to be free and roam about in their kingdom. "Apart from the reference to the *Pooyas* dating back to 33 AD, *Cheitharol Khumbaba* records that in the year 186 Sakabda (AD 264), Meidungu Taothingmang, a *Kuki* became king (Haokip, 2008, p. 6). King of Manipur would mean the existence of many of his tribe men and women for support and warfare. The *Kukis* of Manipur heavily depended on swidden cultivation, which was a sign of their ownership of vast land in and around their settlement. In the village context, this mode of cultivation continues to date. Every move of an indigenous *Kuki's* life from the mother's womb to the grave is governed by customs, rituals, with specific rules and regulations (Haokip, 2008). The *Kukis* are known as fierce warriors, good singers, decked with linguistic proverbs, jokes, idioms that communicate great lessons in a short sentence or a phrase.

2.1.1. Origin of the *Kukis*, Shelter, Clothing

The origin of the indigenous *Kukis* is still shrouded with mythologies and tales. One such interesting traditional accounts that had been handed down through generations says that the *Kukis* came out of the bowels of the earth or a cave called 'Chinlung' or 'Sinlung' or 'Khul', the location of which was believed by some to be somewhere in China. But, others claimed it to be in Tibet (Gangte, 2010). Zawla, a Mizo historian, claimed that the *Kukis* came out of the Great Wall of China in about 225 BC, during the reign of *Shih Hungti* whose cruelty was then at its height (Gangte, 2010). In the book, Zale'n-Gam: The Kuki Nation, P. S. Haokip (2008) states, the *Kukis* are found living in the present-day "Northeast India, Northwest Burma and the Chittagong Hill Tracts of Bangladesh. The *Kukis* lived in this part of the Indian sub-continent without being separated by international boundaries up until the early part of the twentieth century" (p. 1). They were an independent loving group of people with numerous customs and traditions which they hold dear to their heart till today. The *Kukis* are a group of indigenous people who see hierophany, i.e., the manifestation of the sacred absolutely everywhere (Chongloi, 2008). They like to travel within their given country in search of fertile land with thick forests for rice cultivation and hunting wild animals. Indigenous *Kukis* resisted the mighty Britishers when forced to work. Haokip (2015) who had the rare chance to visit British Library, London, UK, exposes an unalterable document found in the Despatch on the Operations against the *Kuki* Tribes of Assam and Burma, November 1917 to March 1919, File No. 4895, Field Operations, Simla, from Lieutenant-General Sir J.D'U. Keary, K.C.B., K.C.I.E., D.S.O., L.A., General Officer Commanding, Burma Division, No. 1762-K.P.M., dated Maymyo, June 1919, to The Chief of the General Staff Army Headquarters, India, Simla, (Diary No. 69190), states, "It is not for me to discuss the cause of the revolt, beyond saying that it was the outcome of a strong objection amongst the hillmen to being sent overseas in Labour Corps" (p. 36). Lieutenant-General Sir J.D'U. Keary's plan of action further read, "I, therefore, decided to put an end to the *Kuki* revolt by force of arms, break the *Kuki* spirit, disarm the *Kukis*, exact reparation and pave the way for an effective administration of their country" (p. 36). Even the British, the then most powerful conquerors, referred about the *Kuki* country where the latter reigned independently. The resistance, when forced into Labour Corps, was a clear sign of their independent nature in their own country. Given the resistance put up by the *Kukis*, Haokip (2015) replicates what Brigadier-General C.E.K. Macquoid, D.S.O., General Officer Commanding, wrote about *Kuki* Punitive Measures, thus:

> The disturbed country to be subjugated covered an area some 6,000 square miles in extent with a Kuki population roughly estimated at 40,000. The whole of this area is covered with hills rising from 2,600 to over 9,000 feet in height. These hills, in turn, are covered with dense forest and jungle, through which run no roads, and paths and jungle tracks are few. With the exception of hill rice, no local supplies are to be obtained therein. (p. 55)

Against the present geographical area of Manipur which is "22,327 square kilometres" (Barbara, Stanley, & Deryck, 2018), 15540 square kilometres (6,000 square miles) was considered *Kuki* country. It needs no description than to say the *Kuki* country was large. A further description of the disturbed country, was divided into the following six areas: "(1) North-East: Somra and North Chassad, (2) East: Chassad, (3) South-East: Mombi and Longya, (4) South: Manhlung, (5) South-West: Hinglep and Ukha, (6) North-West: Silchar Road and Jampi" (Haokip, 2015, p. 55).

For the indigenous *Kukis*, the plentiful expressions of culture and tradition since their ancestors' time are unique, interesting, festive, communitarian, and impressive when the implicated nuances are known. Various scholars and British colonialist officials broadly describe the *Kukis* as belonging to the Mongolian stock (Haokip, 2008). The researcher uses the word 'Kuki' to signify the *Thadou* dialect speaking community of the indigenous *Kukis* of Manipur state (Chongloi, 2013).

Shaw (1929) said, "There is one point that makes me suppose that they (Kukis) must have been previously either ocean-shore, creek, river or lake-bank dwellers. They build their houses on piles and do not live on the ground like the Nagas (excepting the Aos). Until today, the majority of indigenous *Kukis* in the villages still do not like to live on the ground. Even the poorest person wants his house raised above the ground with wood or bamboo floor. This could be because of the cold floor, wet floor, non-availability of even ground sufficient for a house built, or a mindset inherited from their ancestors.

The *Kuki* men wore a loincloth called "Del" which is worn somewhat like a "Dhoti" and have one or more clothes to wrap around themselves over one shoulder or both. They also wear a "Pugri" about a yard or a little longer. It is usually tied around the head with the ends or one end sticking up in front (Shaw, 1929). The *Kuki* men bear features of a Mongolian race. Similar to the Jewish culture, the matured men folk wore long hair tied in a knot at the nape called tuhcha. *Tuhsombem*, a description of hairdo was commonly used to refer to *Kukis* (Haokip, 2008, p. 75). The indigenous sheath (Chempai) bearing a machete (Chempong) was loosely strapped around the waist. Bamboo or cane woven basket called *Paipeh* was used to carry ubiquitous tobacco used by men and women and other food items (Haokip, 2008).

The women wore a loincloth that was wrapped around their waists reaching a little over halfway down their thighs. Attached to the cloth, sometimes separately, a string was passed around the waist to hold it up. Besides, they wore a breast cloth wrapped tight around the torso, the outer corner being tucked in at the top between the left breast and the armpit. At times, an additional wrapper was thrown over the shoulder, thus completing the wardrobe of a simple *Kuki* woman (Shaw, 1929). Haokip (2008) beautifully describes the long-gone *Kuki* woman's usual attire in these words:

> The *Kuki* women wear a knee-length *ponve*, a type of lungi or wrap-around. *Ponve* is wrapped from above the breasts with one end tucked-in under the left arm. A string at the waist fastens a petticoat named *Nih* of red and black stripes. *Khi* or necklace made of red and blue beads was a popular adornment. The hair was properly greased with animal fat, neatly combed, braided in two strands parted at the centre and brought round either side for the head and knotted above the forehead. A woman skilled in weaving was highly prized and sought after for a wife by eligible men. Every Kuki girl, therefore, learnt the skill of weaving. (p. 76)

The wrappers used by men and women may be white or dark indigo blue. The white ones usually have one black band at the extremities (Shaw, 1929). Today, this wrapper or shawl is called

"Mangvom" meaning "blacked fringes." The blue ones have some embroidery in place of those bands.

2.1.2. Beginning of Enmity Between Humans and Spirits

The enmity between humans and spirits arose due to loss of life and value attached to that loss. The mythical ancestors of *Kukis* were known as *Manmasinao* and all spirits were addressed as *Thillha*. They lived in peace until the following incident happened after which the *Thillha* and *Manmasinao* were enemies forever until today. A *Thillha* came to play with a *Manmasinao* called *Changkhatpu*. While playing, *Changkhatpu* lost his temper and wounded the *Thillha* with a dao in his hand. On this, the *Thillha* said *Manmasinao* should suffer for it and escaped to his cave in the jungle. In revenge, during the absence of *Changkhatpu*, *Thillhas* killed his sister. In retaliation, *Manmasinaos* pursued and killed all the *Thillhas* except a pregnant woman *Thillha* who escaped. She went to *Pathen* in the skies and pleaded for help. *Pathen* told her not to worry as the child in her womb is a male child whom she should marry to revive the population of *Thillhas. Pathen* also gifted her a charm called "Chollaivom" instructing her to place it at the water source of the *Manmasinaos* and thereby upon drinking that water, they would not be able to see the *Thillhas* again (Shaw, 1929).

Later, *Japhal*, the daughter of *Kimchal*, the son of *Hangshing* (younger brother of Thadou) got lost one day. All suspected the hands of *Thillhas* in this matter. Her parents wept bitterly at the loss of *Japhal* and invoked the help of *Pathen*. This was one of the myths narrated by Shaw (1929), relating to human suffering of death and losing someone dear. Referring to suffering, Warrington (2006) wrote, "It has been a quest for centuries to try to discover a rationale for it. However, the New Testament while not providing a comprehensive explanation of suffering, does portray the Spirit as having a central role in the life of the believer who suffers" (p. 24). The role of spirit comes into the picture of indigenous *Kuki* life. One night, in *Kimchal's* dream, *Pathen* appeared to him and directed him to take the thing He (Pathen) has placed on the *Sithing* near his house. *Pathen* also asked him to perform sacrifices so that *Kimchal* would beget more descendants and he may not feel the loss of *Japhal*.

He got up and found the *Indoi* (Shaw, 2019, p. 41) which could be translated as "the House God" (Shaw, 1929, p. 41). Therefore, *Kukis* would mount the *Indoi* on the veranda of the house to the right or left of the entrance door, up near the roof out of harm's way (Shaw, 1929). Further, Shaw (1929) has minutely recorded the mention of various elements of nature stuffed together in the *Indoi* or *Doibom*, and the official blessings of *Thempu* at *Indoi* installation, stating:

> Bless him as you blessed the *Gopichengnampha* (the bamboo), *Vomguipha* (the creeper), *Vohpimaikem* (the pig), *Kelchalkihe'* (the goat), *Pengjompa* (the round gourd), *Hailhipha* (the long guard), *Chemkolpha* (the old dao), *Tengmunpha* (the spear), *Chaoveipha* (the wristlet), *Khaopithosom* (the tree whose bark makes rope), *A'tolngo* (the white fowl) and the *Katuilungtheng Katui lungva* (the clean and clear egg). (p. 74)

The author continues to state that, "The Thempu then carries on the blessing prayer that the householder may have many sons and daughters, riches and power and long life" (p. 74). The *Indoi* was expected to bring prosperity and blessings to have a large family. The *Thempu* was the one who would install the *Indoi* in every complete family, where the husband, wife and children were alive and socially upright. The guardian spirit reached the homes of men. Enmity created between humans and spirits led to the institution of *Indoi* or *Doibom,* thus the indigenous religion began.

2.1.3. Indigenous Religion

The indigenous religion of the *Kukis* is what the anthropologists would call "animism" (Changsan, 1992, p. 98). "Near the end of the nineteenth century, an Englishman named Edward Taylor (1832-1917) decided that the beliefs of primitive tribes in a multitude of spirits needed a name. He used the word "animism," from the Latin word 'anima', meaning soul or spirit" (Barnes, 2000, pp. 16-17). Animism is the belief that all nature is animated and that it has a soul, which is detachable from wherever it is lodged in (Chongloi, 2008). After the indigenous *Kukis* accepted Christianity from the West, it has become an immensely difficult task to experience the indigenous religious life. Nonetheless, the researcher honestly attempts to provide the readers dependable information regarding the "basic beliefs of the traditional Kuki religion" (Changsan, 1992) with a special role played by the *Thempu*. This *Thempu* culture might not be the best in the world but it may have been the best to the then indigenous *Kukis* as all the rituals and ceremonies were conducted in their dialect, a sound close to their hearts along with the sacrificial elements available in their surroundings. There is a profoundly established intimate and intricate link between language, life and culture (Joseph, 2017) which remain the medium of correlatedness and communication.

The indigenous *Kukis* believed in the existence of the soul in a human body and other animate and inanimate things. This belief in soul affected many facets of religious practices in the form of rituals at various occasions.

2.1.3.1. Concept of God

Even before the introduction of western Christianity and its accompanying myriad traditions, the indigenous *Kukis* already believed "that *Chung Pathen* (Heavenly God) is the Creator and Sustainer of all trees of the forest and plants of the fields, the waters of the rivers and of the seas, the birds of the air and the animals on the ground, and the illuminaries of the sky" (Changsan, 1992, p. 99). It is also worth to note - while the common *Kuki* term for God is *Pathen*, the Supreme God is often categorically called *Chung Pathen*, meaning, 'God of above', 'High God', 'Supreme God', 'Sovereign God', 'Almighty God' (Changsan, 1992, p. 99). Reverence to God has been an inherited trait.

The indigenous *Thempu* made many incantations invoking the help of *Chung Pathen*. The *Kukis'* belief in the Supreme God is evident in the following incantation pronounced by the priest at the time of cereal offering ritual, "*Nang ka mimpiju, kachangpiju, chunga Pathen na lhaijin...* (in Thadou-Kuki dialect) which means O you wine which is made from the *Mimpi* and *Changpi*, please pacify the God of heaven" (Changsan, 1992. p. 100).

Another chanting of *Thempu* goes like this "*Pathenin van asemin, lei asemin, thingtin asemin, tuitin asemin* ... (in Thadou-Kuki). The meaning is God created heaven and earth, He created all types of trees and water" (Changsan, 1992. p. 100). *Chung Pathen* was the supreme over life on earth.

2.1.3.2. Indoi or Doibom

Learning about *Indoi* practice without knowing the myths behind its origin would be an incomplete knowledge about the indigenous *Kuki* society. The term "myth" comes from the Greek word *muthos,* meaning a tale. Myths are cultural, sacred stories that we tell expressing fundamental "truth" about ourselves in relation to the world around us (Greenberg, 2018, p. 3). A myth may not be literally accepted but nevertheless communicates a reason for an action. As already discussed in the preceding pages, the important reason for the institution of *Indoi* was aimed at begetting children, a sign of God's blessing. Because of this understanding, the rituals for pregnant women, ritual at birth, *Lhalho, Lhakou* became prominent rituals.

Letkhojam Haokip (2000), in his book "Thempuho Thu" stated *Doibom* as a way of ancestral *Kuki* worship before they accepted Christianity. Just like Catholicism is centred around Jesus in the Tabernacle, so also *Pathen* and His powers were centred around *Indoi or Doibom.* Components of *Indoi* were "pig's skull, the curled horn of he-goat, gourd, king of the bamboos, cord made from fiber plant" (Chongloi, 2008, ixx). All these show the harmony of flora and fauna of that particular setting. *Indoi* also explicitly hinted the ever-presence of *Pathen* or Supreme Being who cares, watches, protects humans from evil spirits. The *Thempu* was always needed during the festivals and rituals such as *Lhalho, Chang-Ai, Sa-Ai, Chon, Khopi Kilhaina, Phunsan,* Marriage, Death, War, *Indoi,* (Haokip, 2000). The prime reason for the existence of *Indoi* was to show respect and value the human body in the form of birth, fertility and continuance of generation. *Indoi,* in a way, fructified marriage or was believed to fructify marriage. One cannot be stuck to the symbol of *Indoi* but should carefully see what the symbol signifies. This value accorded to the human body will continue at the ritual of *Sanglai Tun* even after death, at burial, and concept of life after death. "Be fruitful and multiply" (Gen 1:28a) was God's blessing upon humankind. Further, it becomes sensible to read the first account of creation in the Bible, "God saw everything that he had made, and indeed, it was very good" (Gen 1:31a). *Indoi* indeed became a symbol for continuity of generation and human's dependence on God for prosperity and fertility.

Greenberg (2018) writes, "Christian thinkers understand and interpret the Book of Genesis as the basis of what is known as the fall of humanity and the doctrine of original sin" (p. 8). If the Genesis story of God interacting with human became a basis of fall, the contact of God with humans in the *Indoi* symbol became *Kukis'* first instance of obedience and allegiance to God. If the sin of Adam and Eve have brought separation with God, the *Indoi* can be viewed as a redeeming symbol for connection with God. From the Biblical perspective, communication in dreams was considered valid and important. Dreams communicated divine symbols or God himself. For instance, we have the dreams of two prisoners "We have had dreams, and there is no one to interpret." And Joseph said to them, "Do not interpretations belong to God? Please tell them to me" (Gen 40:8). In the New Testament, God's revelation to humankind was confirmed to Joseph in a dream thus, "Get up, take the child and his mother, and flee to Egypt and remain there until I tell you; for Herod is about to search for the child, to destroy him" (Matt 2:13). Obedience of the New Testament Joseph led to the realization of God's plan of salvation for humanity through Jesus Christ. Similarly, God's communication to *Kimchal* in a dream and the latter's subsequent obedience to God brought about the institution of *Indoi* in the indigenous *Kuki* culture. *Indoi* became a hope for good health and posterity, giving the *Thempu*, his vital role at every installation.

2.1.3.3. Thempu

The *Kuki* traditional form of priesthood is called *Thempu*. The word *Thempu* is a combination of two sub-words. "Them" means 'an expert in something specific' and "Pu" is a masculine suffix (Haokip, 1979, p. 60). *Thempu* was an expert in religious concerns and a ritual expert. The *Thempu* of the village was someone considered trustworthy, honest, and interested in the welfare of the people. He had the additional gift of knowing the mind of spirits and *Pathen*

(God). He was a mediator between the human world and the spirit world. There were various roles *Thempu* played and his role seemed indelible on every occasion in the lives of the village people. He was held with regard, awe and fear as he knew something about the spirit world. *Thempu* i.e., the medicine man or soothsayer (Shaw 1929) was the only option for survival and healing when people were thought to be possessed by spirits or attacked by malevolent spirits that are found plenty around the human habitat.

The *Thempu* represented a personality who used "the skill of attending: to listen attentively, alert to the content, feeling, and context of communication; and to respond accurately" (Whitehead & Whitehead, 1981, p. 84). Some of the rituals where *Thempu* was very much prominent and needed were *Hun, Indoi, Phunsan, Gamlahlang, Kholailang, Lhakou, Khopi kilhaina, kithoina kin* (Haokip, 2000), *Kholhim, Chang Lhakou, Sa Lhakou,* (Haokip, 1979). These were moments when he had to recommend the village people to God, spirits or perhaps request the spirits to enter into peace with humans. He took this work not as a privilege but as a humble instrument for the welfare of the people.

At the birth of any child, the *Thempu* had to perform certain rituals for the smooth, quick and safe delivery of the child. He was expected to perform the ritual of *Kilhakouna* for the newborn child, seeking the protection of ancestral spirits (Haokip, 1979) from the malevolent spirits. This ritual was to bind the spirit of the child with its body to ensure prosperity in the loving arms of his or her parents. Barren couples or women prone to frequent miscarriages sought the help of *Thempu* for a ritual known as "Cha Lhakou" meaning "calling for the soul of a child" (Haokip, 1979, p. 62). This was a way of praying for the fertility of the barren couple or the woman.

The *Thempu* used clay images for sacrifices to appease spirits. The sacrificial "images suggest the interconnectedness of humanity and the earth, and the cyclical nature of all life" (Greenberg, 2018, p. 4). The word "Adam is close to two other Hebrew words, *Adama* which means soil or ground; and *Dam* which means blood" (Greenberg, 2018, p. 5). Symbolic clay-made sacrifices signify the power of earth, clay, dust to redeem humans from sicknesses. Just like the clay human came to life with the breath of God, the clay animals were considered alive with the chant of indigenous *Thempu*. These animals and priced possessions were offered to spirits in exchange for the soul of the sick person. For all the works he did for the villagers, he was given a portion of meat, called *Themsa* which is "the upper portion of flesh on the spine" (Haokip, 2008, p. 77). The *Thempu* was expected to memorize longs chants. The oral tradition was kept up through long ritual chants.

2.2. Oral Traditions

Myths surrounding the indigenous *Kuki* culture spring from ages of oral tradition. They can be read as "an etiological story, meaning reading the story as reflecting the prevalent social order at the time of its composition" (Greenberg, 2018 p. 6). These myths originated before the *Kukis* learnt reading and writing any script. "Creation myths" (Greenberg, 2018, p. 3) are methods of connecting metaphysical and physical realities in a given culture. These oral myths also give us an area of existence as humans – what we are in the cosmos.

The indigenous *Kukis* believed that they came from a cave. After *Chongthu* had escaped from the cave, he begot a son, named *Sattong* who was later married to *Sheichin* of *Vanlai* (the Sky) village. It was said that *Sheichin* would go regularly to her father's place to bring pork for her husband. However, her first three attempts were frustrated by *Santhuh Kaoshe*. *Sattong* became so enraged at the behaviour of *Santhuh Kaoshe*, so he went and beheaded him. However, two *Chil* (blindworms) ate up a piece of his neck and thereby brought *Santhuh Kaoshe* back to life again. In place of being a "mythical king, he was transformed into a *guldu* (Hylobates hoolock) and so *Thadous* do not eat the flesh of the gibbons" (Shaw, 1929, p. 40).

The *Thempu* closely observed how the blindworms (Chil) brought *Santhuh Kaoshe* back to life again. By learning the technique, have established the art of performing sacrifices in cases of wounds where blood loss occurs, and thereby saved the lives of many (Shaw, 1929). It was believed, until then, the *Thempu* was able to see the *Thillhas* with his naked eyes. He did learn from the *Thillhas* some good things about the healing of ailments.

Immediately after *Sattong* beheaded *Santhuh Kaoshe*, he became very ill with throat pain and almost died. At that time his faithful dog having compassion on his suffering, licked his hand. *Sattong* was enraged and killed his dog with his sword. The blood of the dog spurted out on *Sattong's* mouth and he was miraculously cured instantly. During the time of *Thempus*, in cases of serious illness, a dog was sacrificed to the creator (Pathen) to relieve the sufferings of the sick (Shaw, 1929). Although *Thempu* was a religious man, he nevertheless had a prominent status in the village administration too.

2.3. Village Administration

In the indigenous *Kuki* society, the chief runs the village affairs with his council of ministers called *Semang-Pachong* in which the *Thempu* had a prominent role. Further uncovering the indigenous *Kuki* society, Haokip (2008) describes the usual annual assembly of an indigenous *Kuki* village community held at the chief's residence called as the *Inpi* (Assembly). He further recounts, in such an *Inpi*, the chief and his *Semang-Pachong* and all the household heads of the village gather to deliberate and resolve matters relating to the village and the community. Most of the decisions were commonly decided with the council of ministers and heads of each clan as representatives. Women were hardly included in decision-making. Women were expected to serve wine to men during meetings, feasts, rituals. Although, there is modest respect shown to women, the patriarchal atmosphere continues even up to this day.

2.3.1. *Haosa* and Land Ownership

The *Kukis* have a social system called chieftainship. "The *Kuki Haosa* or chieftain system of administration embodies the core of *Kuki* polity and is the epitome of *Kuki* custom and tradition" (Haokip, 2008, p. 73). The chief is the ultimate owner of the village land and the people who live in his village are just ordinary and temporary settlers who pay yearly tribute as a mark of their allegiance to him. The eldest son of the chief becomes the inheritor after his father. In case, the chief does not beget a son of his own, the village land will pass on to the younger brother of the reigning chief. "MacCrea described them as a nation of hunters and warriors, rules as a nation by their principal hereditary Chiefs or Raja, but divided into clans, each under its own chiefs" (Haokip, 2008, p. 3). In Manipur, amongst the indigenous *Kukis*, it is interesting to see the customary laws functioning alongside the secular laws within the democratic framework (Kipgen, 2012) of the Indian Constitution. All people living in a particular village become subjects to the chief as he is the head of the local government, and only by moving away or migration could they escape his control. Outsiders cannot settle in the village territory without the chief's permission, who rehabilitated them wherever he wishes (Gangte, 2010).

With almost unquestionable power in the village, the *Haosa* becomes a symbol of unity and security in the indigenous *Kuki* society. Haokip (2008) opines, "The *Haosa* has the responsibility to provide security to his villagers socially, politically and economically. All Legislative, Executive and Judicial powers are vested in him" (p. 73). Even unto this day, the *Haosa* is the head of indigenous *Kuki* village. He can be a boon or a bane as well depending on his ability and educational background.

2.4. Rituals

In the indigenous *Kuki* society, rituals were conducted by the *Thempu* on many important occasions or otherwise conducted by the man of the house in certain small rituals. Ritual can be termed as an activity that has human in its mode but has the invisible God as its more than a human agent (Bouyer, 1999). Here, we find an embryonically contained fact that "ritual is a human action coincident with the divine, namely that man is not merely a microcosm but is an image of the divine" (Bouyer, 1999, p. 14). The belief that "God created humankind in his image, in the image of God he created them, male and female he created them" (Gen 1:27) evokes relevance and honour.

Rituals were also occasions for the indigenous *Kukis* to remember their ancestral names. Shaw (1929) documents, "They specially pride themselves on genealogical trees which play importance in some of their rituals and festivities" (p. 22). The various rituals of the *Kukis* express the influence of supernaturalism. As their society was based on the traditional beliefs of the land, it included a variety of myths and folklore which were chanted through prayers on various occasions around the year. However, the rituals of indigenous *Kuki*s do not make mention of any sacred place which can be treated best for rituals. Each ritual had a different setting and items for the sacrificial offering. Since the supernatural God was believed to be omnipresent, almost every place was considered good. To a certain degree, the *Kukis* had accepted the world as a sacrament of communion, as a way of sharing with God and neighbour (F S, 2017) because of which they considered the spirits inhabit the world. They did not claim the world as a personal belonging. Rather, they shared and lived with their fellow men, treating the world as a means for livelihood. Feasts and festivals stand as witnesses to this outlook in their lives. Most of the rituals were agro-based as the people primarily depended on agriculture for their survival and success in life. At the time of marriage too, rituals were conducted to invoke blessings and promise commitment.

2.4.1. Marriage

In a way, marriage can be considered as the beginning of rituals that necessitates other rituals like marital ritual itself, rituals from birth to death. Marriage was a sign of entering into maturity and responsibility. Marriage became a way of expanding one's associations with others through marital relationships. Fertility and begetting many children were perceived as God's abundant blessing. Haokip (2017) points out about the indigenous *Kuki* tradition in marriage, thus:

> In the traditional *Kuki* society, monogamy and endogamy are the dominant forms of marriage while polygamy is not practiced although there are rare cases. Exogamy was not permitted and polyandry is not heard of in the *Kuki* Society. There are different types of marriages among the *Kukis* by which a mate/partner is acquired, such as *chongmou a kipui, sahap sat a kipui, jol lhah a kicheng, kijam a kicheng,* and *jol gai a kicheng.* The first two are arranged marriages while the rests amount to the type of love marriage by elopement. (p. 274)

The institution of marriage gave further consideration of the value of life. Other indigenous *Kuki* rituals focusing on body and soul at birth, during childhood, good fortune, sickness, death, originate from marriage and family life. Every ritual was strictly guarded during one's lifetime, a sign of allegiance to that society. At the end of human existence the indigenous *Kuki* concept of life after death continues in the form of *Mithi Kho*. The *Thempu* played an important role in minutely conducting death ritual to envisage entry of the soul of the dead person into the next life where dead ancestors were thought to dwell. It can even be termed as *Kuki* eschatological concept. Life was thought to be here on earth and the next. This firm belief had prompted the indigenous *Kukis* to offer food at the grave as if the dead still needed physical food. Deeds during life here on earth were thought to have effects after death. The concept of life after death prompted them for upright behaviour while they were on this earthy existence.

2.4.2. Concept of Life After Death

The indigenous *Kukis* firmly believed in the existence of the soul in every human being and every created thing on earth. The term for soul is *lha* or *thilha*. The term "Soul" is described in *Kuki* language of as "Lhagao" in the poetical form (Haokip, 2006). The *Kukis* believed that after death, the soul was to pass through *Lhanpelkot* and *Thijonbung*, through which place all the souls or spirits of the dead have to pass on their way to *Mithi Kho*, the village of the dead (Shaw, 1929). An old witch was thought to be guarding that village and whoever passes by she would make them her slave. The witch would force dead women to look for lice on her head and eat them as well. This woman, however, would not separate man and woman who truly love each other. They believed that the animals killed and eaten during *Chon le Han* would accompany them when they die and pass through *Mithi Kho*. When someone died, they would kill his or her dog and bury along with him or her. The dog was supposed to accompany the dead and open the gates of *Mithi Kho*.

When my grandfather (Joseph Helkhokhai), who was an indigenous *Kuki Thempu* died on the 13th December 2013, the family dog (Tyson) that was with him for about five years, also died a few minutes later. Elders interpreted my grandfather as a renounced *Thempu,* who even a dog sensed and followed him. When big Chiefs or people of prominence died, their slaves were sacrificed and buried together to serve them in the next life too. The belief in next life was strongly held although they might not have had any idea about the Christian concept of resurrection of the dead. The dead ancestors were thought to be up high in heaven protecting the living descendants. The *Thempu* reiterates the belief in next life through the ritual of the dead. An instance may clarify. As the mud was refilled in the grave after the coffin has been laid down, the *Thempu* would insert a bamboo stick or rope inviting the soul of the dead out of the grave towards heavenly abode. The belief was that only the physical body should lie in the grave and the soul out of the body.

Conclusion

The research period was an occasion to go beyond what meets the human eye. It was a retrospective journey of about 100 years to see come alive indigenous *Kuki* ancestors with their given theological understanding of God and nature. The themes of relationality; constant effort for the alleviation of human suffering and pain through rituals; a sense of worth; the experience of God's ever presence in *Indoi* were some significant pointers for further deliberation. The indigenous *Kukis* enjoyed creative and redemptive ways of God in their ordinary life setting. The redeeming nature of God was already felt through the *Thempu's* conduct of rituals for healing and wellbeing.

The research was worth it. From the researcher's limited experiences and the vast experiences of the interviewees, one can conclude that an indigenous *Kuki* theology was already there during the *Thempu* era. The sense of trust on the all-powerful God was manifested in all rituals. Revelations of God in dreams, followed by unconditional obedience is both biblical and theologically sound. The *Indoi* symbol can serve as a sign of obedience to God's revelation and pathway for posterity.

This approach would naturally set aside the imported, alien and forced upon westernized Christianity. The question today is "Can the indigenous *Kukis* be Christians with their culture?" "Can the

Kuki indigenous rituals and symbols be theologized from a Christian perspective for richer interaction?" The researcher is encouraged for better pastoral management and inclusive ministry of the wisdom of ancestors entwined with Catholic priesthood.

The rediscovery of one's indigenous worldview of life is a need. Anything to be successful should take foundational root from its noble indigenous practices that can lead the society forward to betterment. The rich and indigenous heritage handed down through custom and culture can be rediscovered and relived in Christian life. Although "sancritisation of the plain area have been going on for centuries" (Raatan, 2001, p. 12) in Manipur, the indigenous *Kukis* and the traditional primal priesthood seemed to hold a strong ground within their culture. As such, there are no indigenous *Kukis* who have converted to Hinduism or being affected adversely by sancritisation.

The indigenous *Kukis* were God-fearing people even before the coming of western Christianity. The social values of respect, truthfulness, love, integrity, non-manipulation were at high regard then than now. Though western Christian English education is appreciated, one cannot accept all the values that came along with it.

The sense of trust in God was present amongst the indigenous *Kukis*. The sense of holiness and sacredness of every person was seen in rituals conducted by the *Thempu*. The psychology, spirituality, emotional, social, relational aspects of the indigenous *Kukis* were seen in their trust on the *Thempu* who would, but do something good for them.

While the village chief was for the material governance of the village, *Thempu* was entrusted with the spiritual or Godly aspects of life. Marriage prompted the necessity of many other rituals thereby binding people and building inter-familial networks. Interference of malevolent spirits into the lives of human necessitated firm belief in *Pathen*. The third chapter attempts to describe the dynamics of integrating indigenous *Thempu* ethos with the Catholic priesthood.

Chapter 3

Integrating *Thempu* Ethos with the Catholic Priesthood

Introduction

Upon close observation and reflection, one can detect there are intricately knitted connections between indigenous *Thempu* tradition and Catholic priesthood in its concepts and actual practice. By bringing in indigenous *Thempu* tradition, the researcher is neither encouraging controversy nor inviting division. It is an attempt to situate one in the other and find effective practicality in pastoral ministry.

A sense of rootedness and a healthy knowledge of one's culture and custom will augment acceptance and deeper reflection of other traditions around the world. Firstly, I was born in an indigenous *Kuki* community. Secondly, my parents introduced me to Christianity. They are in a way, my first and second identities.

The then practice of indigenous *Thempu* tradition was in a particular culture and language whereas Catholic priesthood has existed in multicultural audiences. Indigenous *Thempu* and Catholic priests invariably attend to the needs of people from birth (or even before birth) to death (even after death).

Invoking ancestors or saints give persons a chance of witnessing in one's life. Taking the names of ancestors or saints inspires and challenges people towards life worthy of the acquired name. Indigenous traditions and religious traditions do not stand antagonistic but complement each other when the nuances of both are properly explained, researched and understood. Symbolic actions convey the depth of belief and ultimately create unison in family or society. Indigenous *Thempu* and Catholic priests use symbolic elements to convey God's blessings to uphold the sanctity of life and continually intercede for people through their vocations to serve. The respect conferred to human life indicates respect to the originator of life – God.

3.1. Respect for Life

Much before the promulgation of the Encyclical Letter *Humanae Vitae* (1986) by Pope Paul VI, indigenous *Kuki Thempu* and *Kuki* culture already had a placed respect for life in the womb of a woman. Rituals were performed for the good health of the child in the woman's womb and safe delivery. Even an additional *Sa-o* was attached to her own *Sa-o* (Haokip, 2000). Life was considered a divine gift at every stage of human existence.

3.1.1. Cultic Ritual Prayers for Children

In the indigenous *Kuki* culture, prayers were offered for a child while being still in the womb of the mother. The special ritual called *Nao Juneh/Nao Anneh/Nao Anndop* was also performed for good health at the birth of a child. After children have grown up, along with their parents, they would go to their maternal uncle's home for *Kilhalho*. In the ritual of *Kilhalho*, the child was given a necklace called "Sa-o" – a kind of necklace, made of cotton thread with a chicken feather tightly held (Haokip, 2000, p. 60) as a symbolic sign of God's blessing. *Sa-o* was found in various types. To an outsider, this simple combination of a thread and a chicken feather may look outlandish. However, to an indigenous *Kuki* mind, symbols are real and they signify something beyond what meets the eye.

Seeking *Pathen's* blessings, all these rituals symbolized the interconnectedness of the body and soul of every human person.

Symbolic forms of expression are found in the East rather than the West. In India too, "symbols, symbolic language, myths and stories" (Gonsalves, 2015, p. 49) are often used in various rituals and occasions of life. In the indigenous *Kuki* society, religion and culture were smoothly interwoven. "Religion is somehow *sui generis* and that it should not be understood on its own terms, not reduced to anything else. Otherwise, religion is 'explain away,' or at least the scholar misses what is really important in religion" (Pyysiäinen, 2004, p. 2). Goodwill and blessings of ancestors, maternal uncles' families and *Pathen* were thought to bring health and longevity. This belief "takes cognizance of the interrelation of the divine, the human and the cosmic" (Gonsalves, 2015, p. 52) which is a cosmotheandric approach. Cultural analysis, therefore, is "not an experimental science in search of law but an interpretive one in search of meaning" (Pyysiäinen, 2004, p. 2) from what is observed in a particular culture.

Harmonious existence of the soul and body was highly desired in the indigenous *Kuki* society. Therefore, when the soul (spirit) of someone was treated well, the body was thought to be healthy. This belief makes sense of ritual prayers for children to enhance the health of the body and soul. This ritual brings joy and hope to the expectant mother, induces preparedness in the minds of the family members and introduces a social sense of acceptance to the unborn child. The sense of care and wellbeing brought in social security.

Beyond the rituals performed, the symbolic acts form their perception of God as relational and other-concern. It consolidates responsible parenthood and acceptance of children as a gift of God. The Encyclical, *Humanae Vitae* says, "the exercise of responsible parenthood requires that husband and wife, keeping a right order of priorities, recognize their own duties toward God, themselves, their families and human society" (Paul VI, 1968, no.10). The right order of priorities in the instance of indigenous rituals for the unborn showed respect to the indigenous age-old custom, acceptance of conjugal union, reception of the unborn child as God's gift, and reverence shown to the unborn child. According to Paul VI's *Humanae Vitae* (1968) "fundamental nature of the marriage act, while uniting husband and wife in the closest intimacy, also renders them capable of generating new life" (no. 12) as a gift of God. Remotely, those rituals were acceptance of manhood and womanhood as designed by God. It was also a sign of appreciation to the would-be mother and father. The unitive and procreative aspects of marriage were respected. The sacredness of human life was endorsed. The rituals oriented man and woman to responsible parenthood while expecting help and support from society. From mere ritual performances, they become a communitarian celebration of life and all that surrounds it. These acts become "sacramental moments" (Macquarrie, 1998, p. 12) for this community. Thus, they "lead to new avenues of the understanding of a sacramental spirituality of history and creation" (Haring, 1976, p. 9) handed down by ancestors as a way of appreciation and acceptance of the couple and unborn or newly born child.

Pope Francis in his apostolic letter "To All Consecrated People" (2014) stressed saying, "Recounting our history is essential for preserving our identity, for strengthening our unity as a family and our common sense of belonging" (no. I.1). Therefore, it is wise to develop a theology from the various indigenous rituals, myth, metaphors, practices, beliefs where people can find God in their values and beliefs. This ultimately invites us to dive into the context and build our God experience rather than go with conceptual knowledge of God and test people's beliefs. From human's life experiences, emerge theology, not the other way about. Ordinary elements of nature can be given sacramental tag when accepted with faith.

3.1.2. Catholic Rituals at Baptism

Christian initiation of human beings could be concretely seen at the ritual of baptism. Keenan (2005) marks, "The body is central for understanding Christianity. Through the body we understand God, our worship, our destiny, and our communal identity" (p. 54). The ritual of Christian baptism, acknowledging the preciousness of the body to enter into a relationship with other members of the church speaks about the graciousness of God in the human body. This is a "celebration of faith and of hope in the community of salvation in Christ. We experience in baptism our personal insertion into the new and eternal covenant, as members of the chosen people"

(Haring, 1976, p. 139). In the words of Gonsalves (2015) "Catholics believe that baptism immerses us into the salvific streams of Christ's death-and-resurrection, our *Pascha*, makes us a 'new creation' and washes away our 'original sin'" (p. 216). It serves as an entry into a relationship with God and other members of the Church. John Paul II, in *Donum Vitae* (1987), stressed on the sacredness of life saying, "Human life is sacred because from its beginning it involves 'the creative action of God' and it remains forever in a special relationship with the Creator, who is its sole end" (no. 18). Whether one believes in "Augustinian notion of original sin, connecting it with heredity and sexuality" (Macquarrie, 1998, p. 67), sin does not seem to be absent in the human society. To believe that there is no sin and we have no sin may be the surest way to be a liar. For "If we say that we have no sins, we deceive ourselves, and the truth is not in us" (1 Jn 1:8). Baptism, as a sacrament, initiates us to live like Christ.

Prayer for an infant in the sacrament of Baptism becomes a direct symbol of appreciation and involvement in the upbringing of the child. Priests and people who participate in this ritual vouch goodwill and moral support to the baptized-child. According to John Paul II, in *Familiaris Consortio* (1981), "Since God's plan for marriage and the family touches men and women in the concreteness of their daily existence in specific social and cultural situations, the Church ought to apply herself to understanding the situations within which marriage and the family are lived today, in order to fulfill her task of serving" (no. 4). Gal 3:27 reads, "Many of you were baptized into Christ have clothed yourselves with Christ." Baptism becomes a symbolic and public acceptance of Christ. St Paul further reiterates when he says, "So if anyone is in Christ, there is a new creation: everything old has passed away; see, everything has become new" (2 Cor 5:17). The ultimate command of Jesus to his disciples stand out as a mandate to be fulfilled, "Go therefore and make disciples of all nations, baptizing them in the name of the Father, and of the Son and of the Holy Spirit" (Matt 28:19).

Just as Holy Orders is a vocation to the ministerial priesthood, so also marriage is a sacrament of vocation to love, love without measure. The encyclical letter *Humanae Vitae* (1968) of Paul VI exhorts "Christian husbands and wives be mindful of their vocation to the Christian life, a vocation which, deriving from their Baptism, has been confirmed anew and made more explicit by the Sacrament of Matrimony" (no. 25). The sacrament of baptism for a newborn child becomes a sign of blessing after a man and a woman have maturely decided for the sacrament of marriage. The bearing of children and childbirth is a sure sign of God's blessing of progeny. Therefore, "the Church once again feels the pressing need to proclaim the Gospel, that is the 'good news,' to all people without exception, in particular to all those who are called to marriage and are preparing for it, to all married couples and parents in the world" as encouraged by John Paul II in *Familiaris Consortio* (1981, no. 3). Marriage remains a sacred institution in the Catholic Church for the continuation of humankind, which is a sign of God's manifold blessings. Rituals are symbols of God's participation in the lives of human beings.

3.2. Catholic Priests

Catholic priests are men who have willingly accepted to serve God and people in the ministerial priesthood of Christ. They are people specially chosen for the service of the word of God and sacraments. Podimattam, (2008) stresses "The relationship with God remains key in the life of priests. Priesthood does indeed require skill, competence, hard work and discipline" (p. 15). For the fruitful service to people, priests need to have a firm relationship with God, the source of life and energy for service. They are to connect God, the world and people in their day-to-day existence and experience. It may be interesting to ask, Why do Catholic priesthood exist? Macquarrie (1998) aptly answers the question, thus:

> All have a ministry in the church of Christ, but not all have the same ministry. Within the one body from the beginning there have been distinctive ministries, having special responsibility for the ministry of word and sacraments, and for exercising pastoral oversight; and such ministries also needed a special grace if they were to be rightly exercised. This was the situation that called for a sacrament of orders or ordination. (p. 180)

St Paul, in his first letter to Corinthians, reminds us, "Now there are varieties of gifts, but the same Spirit; and there are varieties of services, but the same Lord; and there are varieties of activities but it is the same God who activates all of them in everyone. To each is given the manifestation of the Spirit for the common good" (12:4-8). In this sense, Catholic priesthood is one of the many varieties of services in the Church. Priests become channels for people to experience God in their given cultural contexts. They initiate a movement towards God to appreciate nature and mutual respect for humanity. Just like a prophet who speaks the mind of God to people, so is the call of Catholic priests.

Ordination to the priesthood is a "lifelong vocation and commitment, and indeed it takes a lifetime for the full formation of a priestly character" (Macquarrie, 1998, p. 182). Generally, a Catholic priest is assigned a community to care or allocated an area to form a community. Here, 'community' refers to people who profess 'same faith.' John Paul II's *Pastores Dabo Vobis* (1992) highlights the need for priests saying, "Without priests, the Church would not be able to live that fundamental obedience which is at the very heart of her existence and her mission in history, an obedience in response to the command of Christ: 'Go therefore and make disciples of all nations' (Matt 28:19) and 'Do this in remembrance of me' (Lk 22:19; cf. 1 Cor 11.24), i.e., an obedience to the command to announce the Gospel and to renew daily the sacrifice of the giving of his body and the shedding of his blood for the life of the world" (no. 1). Making disciples of all nations is to attune every person into the mind of God who has created the world for good. A priest becomes an agent for the continuation of an already formed community that heads towards faith excellence. In a mission area, he becomes a catalyst in gathering, instructing, educating a group of people to form a community of faith. From this faith community, he may move on to form an educational community through the administration of schools, colleges and universities.

A spiritually balanced and intellectual fit priest can be of great service to the Church. The Church invests more than ten years towards the holistic formation of a person before ordaining him a priest. In his Post-Synodal Apostolic Exhortation, *Pastores Dabo*

Vobis (1992), John Paul II affirms, "Intellectual formation has its own characteristics, but it is also deeply connected with, and indeed can be seen as a necessary expression of, both human and spiritual formation" (no. 51). John Paul II continues stressing in *Pastores Dabo Vobis* (1992) that "A sound philosophy can help candidates for the priesthood to develop a reflective awareness of the fundamental relationship that exists between the human spirit and truth, that truth which is revealed to us fully in Jesus Christ" (no. 52). Philosophy and theology are mandatory subjects in the formation of priests. *Lumen Gentium* of Paul VI (1964) stressed the importance of faith while engaging in theology. He asserted, "True theology proceeds from the faith and aims at leading to the faith. This is the conception of theology which has always been put forward by the Church and, specifically, by her Magisterium. This is the line followed by the great theologians who have enriched the Church's thinking. St. Thomas is extremely clear when he affirms that the faith is as it were the habitus of theology, that is, its permanent principle of operation, and that the whole of theology is ordered to nourishing the faith" (no. 53). Proper education broadens the mind to accommodate cultures one has not seen and experienced so far. Philosophy and theology become necessary pastoral tools for one's future ministry amongst the people.

A Catholic priest becomes a symbol of freedom and progress for common good. Haring (1976), while speaking of liturgy and moral life points out fundamental principles for adherence in pastoral ministry, thus:

1. The genuine priestly and above all the great prophetic traditions, as well as the deepest experiences of people of our secular era, prove that individual persons and communities are not condemned to become slaves of idols, ideologies and tyrants...A genuine renewal, therefore, rejects all forms of alienation, any separation of life and worship.
2. Another form of alienation is that of an ossified cult, a form of worship so rigid as to be incapable of expressing the freshness and newness of the divine messages or of

> communicating it to the world of human hopes. Christ himself sharply and explicitly protested against all those religious forms which had become, for man, a cause of alienation from God and from his neighbour. (p. 7)

3.2.1. Catholic Priestly Consecrated Life

The Post-Synodal Apostolic Exhortation, *Vita Consecrata* (1996) of John Paul II acknowledges that "In every age there have been men and women who, obedient to the Father's call and to the prompting of the Spirit, have chosen this special way of following Christ, in order to devote themselves to him with an undivided heart" (1 Cor 7:34) (no. 1). In his apostolic letter "To All Consecrated People," Pope Francis stressed on the rich history and charisms of the Church saying, "At their origins, we see the hand of God who, in his Spirit, calls certain individuals to follow Christ more closely, to translate the Gospel into a particular way of life, to read the signs of the time with the eyes of faith and to respond creatively to the needs of the Church" (no. I.1).

Catholic priests are consecrated for spreading the gospel in tune with the need of time. John Paul II on *Vitae Consecrata* (1996) puts in perspective stating, "The evangelical basis of consecrated life is to be sought in the special relationship which Jesus, in his earthly life, established with some of his disciples. He called them not only to welcome the Kingdom of God into their own lives but also to put their lives at its service, leaving everything behind and closely imitating his own *way of life*" (no. 14). In "the classic call narratives from scripture – those of Abraham, Moses, Jeremiah, Isaiah, the twelve apostles, and Saint Paul – one sees this pattern merge" (Podimattam, 2008, p. 15), where God initiates a personal contact before sending them out for a mission.

The primary aim of consecrated life is not aloofness but a movement towards God and people "by allowing themselves to be guided by the Spirit on an endless journey of purification, they become, day after day, *conformed to Christ*" (Podimattam, 2008, p. 19). John Paul II's *Vitae Consecrata* (1996) affirmed of the value attached to consecrated life and the many ways of its execution saying, "the consecrated life is at the very heart of the Church as a decisive element for her mission, since it 'manifests the inner nature of the Christian calling' and the striving of the whole Church as Bride towards union with her one Spouse" (no. 3). The core invitation of every Christian is to be with Christ, the spouse of the Church.

The Dogmatic Constitution on the Church, *Lumen Gentium* of Paul VI (1964) accentuated, "The evangelical counsels of chastity dedicated to God, poverty and obedience are based upon the words and examples of the Lord. They were further commanded by the apostles and Fathers of the Church, as well as by the doctors and pastors of souls" (no. 43). Similar to the "totality of giving which is implied in marriage, consecrated chastity expresses vividly the totality of love for God" (Hoffman, 2001, p. 120) which is a spontaneous self-giving. The evangelical counsels of obedience, chastity and poverty beautify consecrated life. Podimattam (2008) brings in the beauty of paradoxes in Christian faith concerning the celibacy of the priests:

> Christian faith proclaims its deepest truths in paradoxes. Like the grain of wheat, we must die in order to find life. We meet Christ in the unlikely guise of the sick and the imprisoned and the stranger. Celibacy is another of our faith's paradoxes. As Christians, we know that we can love one another well apart from genital sharing; we recognize that, even without offspring, we can live fruitful and generous lives. (p. 255)

The central idea of Catholic priestly consecrated life is a firm "union with the Triune God and following Jesus Christ, with an emphasis on one or another aspect of his mission and virtues" (Hoffman, 2001, p. 17). Religious life, like the supernatural life of grace itself, is not meant to crush what is good in human nature but to bring it to perfection" (Hoffman, 2001, p. 26). This good in human nature can be discovered and nurtured through proper ongoing formation. The good in oneself as a priest can also serve students through imparting education. Through service, the flowering of the good in human nature is realized. Spiritual and material growth will fulfil the promise of Jesus who said, "I came that they may have life, and have it abundantly" (Jn 10:10b). Therefore, for a religious to be authentic, following the footsteps of Christ must dominate all other motives and occupations no matter how true, necessary, or relevant they may appear to be (Hoffman, 2001). Christ is the first and the main motif for all priestly undertakings.

Priestly consecrated life is primarily oriented towards others with mercy akin to the heart of Jesus Christ. Followers of Christ who are consecrated as priests stand as witnesses of the divine mercy of God who welcomes all. In *Humanae Vitae* (1968), Paul VI said, "The Church, in fact, cannot act differently toward men than did the Redeemer. She knows their weaknesses, she has compassion on the multitude, she welcomes sinners" (no. 19). Priestly consecrated life becomes an ongoing journey of mercy than condemnation. The letter to Hebrews highlights the expected mercy every high priest is to possess. It reads, "He is able to deal gently with the ignorant and wayward since he himself is subject to weakness" (5:2). A loving priest is often loved more than a legalistic priest who exacts in dealings.

3.2.2. Priestly Services

A priest is conferred the sacerdotal ordination to imitate his master, Jesus, who came not to be served but to serve (Matt 20:28). This service is aimed particularly towards families in the whole of the Catholic Church and to every person. Similar to the Apostles, Catholic priests "have left everything behind in order to be with Christ and to put themselves, as he did, at the service of God and their brothers and sisters," stressed John Paul II in *Vitae Consecrata* (1996, no. 1). Hoffman (2001) stated, "The real world is both spiritual and material, and is reflected in the microcosm that is the human person, who is both body and soul" (p. 14) existent in the society. A priest, a consecrated person, thus necessarily assumes the obligation to care the spiritual and material spheres of people around him.

A Catholic priest functions in a multi-faceted ministry reading the "signs of the time and of interpreting in the light of the Gospel" as exhorted by Paul VI in *Gaudium Et Spes* (1965, no. 4) with relevance and pastoral prudence upholding the teachings of the Church. His spirituality, administrative skills, companionship with people, care for the sick and needy stand out as gifts. He becomes a local visible face of the entire Catholic Church in his liturgical acts, administration of sacraments, sacramentals, social and educational responsibilities entrusted upon him. When he can read the pulse of the people and society, it can be termed as "signs of God's presence and purpose, in the happenings, needs and desires" (Gaudium Et Spes, no. 11) of people around his ministry. He becomes a source of inspiration and channel of encouragement in the joys, sorrows, difficult moments of people under his pastoral care. Sacrament and education are two of the many apostolates in caring for the spiritual and material wellbeing of people in pastoral ministry.

3.2.2.1. Sacraments

God comes to us powerfully in the sacraments so that we can live our lives as He has designed for us. The "approach to the theological foundation of human dignity is of value, and its emphasis on creation and redemption are essential to the Christian story of God's loving care for human beings" (Kelly, 2004, p. 37). Dignity and preciousness of life are augmented in the sacraments of the Church where God powerfully interacts with humankind and provides redemption. "One who does not grasp what signs and symbols are, why we use them, how they function or fail to function and where they lead, is neither likely to understand what sacraments are nor be able to celebrate them meaningfully and effectively" (Gonsalves, 2015, p. 53). One of the multi-faceted ministries of a Catholic priest is to bring life and effectiveness to the sacraments officially espoused by the Holy Catholic Church. Sacraments are symbolic actions of the infinite love of God upon humankind. Gonsalves (2015) quotes the Italian theologian Peter Lombard (approx. 1095-1160) who has been credited with this definition: "A Sacrament is in such a manner an outward sign of inward grace that it bears its image (i.e., signifies or represents it) and is its cause" (p. 108). The author furthers restates, "Sacramentality could be broken up as 'sacra-mentality', referring to the mental ability and inner disposition to perceive all of reality and respond to it as 'sacred' – proceeding from and inseparably united with Ultimate Being whom we call God" (p. 10). When one can perceive the deeper meaning of cultures, customs, rituals of various communities, there is a sense of sacramentality.

Often, there seems to be a distinction but no separation between supernatural revelation and natural events (Haring, 1976) of life.

"Once the full light of Christ has shone, the believer perceives the whole of creation and the ongoing history of mankind in the perspective of God's self-disclosure, of an unfolding manifestation of God's loving design for man" (Haring, 1976, p. 20). Therefore, sacraments of the Church are God's self-manifestation in the life of human beings inviting the latter to be like the former.

The journey of going back to roots, respect for specific cultures and ethos could help to deeply ingrain the Catholic faith in diverse communities. Connecting each sacrament to the various rituals each community already has will be a good start of inculturation and accommodation. This will be a non-threat way to the existing fear of cultural invasion. Spiritualizing and giving a sacramental value to the non-contradictory rituals and prayers of each community or indigenous culture will allow the blossoming of cultural values in the big garden, the Catholic Church. Each uniqueness can add value, beauty and design to the vast landscape of the Church. Identifying mystical beauty in each culture with its diverse fragrance could add to the mosaic of Catholicism. The breadth of tolerance and acceptance of diverse cultures that affiliate to Catholicism is the work of every priest. Rather than mere exalted intellectual concepts and ritualistic adherence, Christifying various cultural ethos will be a more accepted method for 21st century Christianity. Building on what people already have can project the Church as for people and with people. While sacramental administration would restrict to people who officially professed the Catholic faith, education would be a universal service rendered to humankind. Education, aimed at the common good, the growth of every citizen, and special care for the poor would be the mind of Jesus Christ Himself. Education can empower and transform society into a scientific community.

3.2.2.2. Education

Imparting education becomes an important ministry of every Catholic priest. Through education, people belonging to various communities are formed towards holistic growth. The Catholic Bishops' Conference of India (CBCI), the Commission for Education and Culture, in its Vision, Mission and Goals, asserts holistic education of those pupils in Catholic educational institutes.

All India Association for Christian Higher Education affirms of the holistic formation to students:

> Special efforts should be made to enable students: (1) to think for themselves independently and critically; (2) to seek, extend and apply knowledge to the solution of human problems; (3) to continually strive after excellence in every field; (4) to become mature, spiritually aware men and women of character; (5) to value and judiciously use their freedom, combining with it a full sense of responsibility for actions; (6) to be clear and firm on principles and courageous in action; (7) to be unselfish in the service of their fellowmen and concerned for the welfare of the poor and socially oppressed; and (8) to become agents of needed social change in their own situations. (AIACHE Declaration of Purposes, 1982)

Further, CBCI asserts, "The Mission of Jesus Christ is to restore the integrity of God's original creation, both human and material and thus build the Kingdom of God on earth. Our vision is the same as the vision of Jesus - that all may have life and have it in abundance" (Vision, Mission, Goals, no. 2.1). Human and material aspects of building the Kingdom of God can be achieved through holistic education. CBCI shows a cohesive spectrum of education insisting, that education "refines sensitivities and perceptions that contribute to national cohesion, a scientific temper and independence of mind and spirit – thus furthering the goals of socialism, secularism and democracy enshrined in our Constitution" (National Policy on Education, 1986, no. 2.2). CBCI envisages that our Education "enables each student to see his/her life as a gift of God and as a call to serve. We help them to realize that it is right attitudes and principles that give power and dignity to one's life" (A 4.3). Catholic education is to form a person to be a better man and a better woman. The goal of education is not mere orientation towards bread and butter. It emphasizes moral growth, service to the needy, care for the poor and sick.

3.2.2.3. Pastoral Care of the Sick

Jesus, after forming his twelve disciples for few months sent them out with this consoling evidence of his mighty presence to have "power and authority over all demons and to cure diseases and he sent them out to proclaim the kingdom of God and to heal" (Lk 9:2). To heal and restore physical health was one important ministry of Jesus and his first disciples. He was a relevant itinerant preacher of his time. Along with physical cure, Jesus brought in the spirituality of the Jewish scripture and showed the mercy of God. From faith's perspective, "The consequence of being a child of God is that one will suffer (Rom 8:17). However, in that suffering, the power of God is made manifest" (Warrington, 2006, p. 29). Suffering becomes a way of being God's children. Paul's journey to Jerusalem to suffer becomes a means of obeying God through suffering (Acts 21:11).

According to the indigenous *Kuki* culture, sickness and ailments were considered to have arisen with devilish influence and not from God. "Most people in history have considered it self-evident that gods are real, or that the ancestors guide them, or that demons cause sickness" (Barnes, 2000, p. 29). These sicknesses were due to the displeasure of evil spirits or offence against them. The *Thempu* was the only medium for healing and appeasement of spirits that could bring wellbeing of the human community.

In the Catholic Church, the sacrament of 'Anointing of the Sick' is precisely oriented toward physical healing and spiritual nourishment. *Lumen Gentium* by Paul VI (1964) beautifully captures the involvement of the whole Church saying, "By the sacred anointing of the sick and the prayer of her priests the whole Church commends the sick to the suffering and glorified Lord, asking that He may lighten their suffering and save them. She exhorts them, moreover, to contribute to the welfare of the whole people of God by associating themselves freely with the passion and death of Christ" (no. 11). Further, spiritual healing is powerfully brought in if the sick can avail the 'Sacrament of Confession.' Thus, "anointing of the sick signifies the dynamic presence of the Holy Spirit who works in such a way that the faithful can accept the critical hours of illness and of death in the light of the 'final hour,' with peace, without spiritual discomfort or weakening" (Haring, 1976, p. 149). Accompanying the sick at the moment of illness and hour of death is a humbling and rich spiritual experience.

In my pastoral ministry at Sacred Heart Parish, Yairipok, I have experienced various encounters with devil/evil spirits. In one such instance, late at night, I was informed that a boy had been possessed by an evil spirit. This is a Hindu boy, a relative of a Catholic man. I put on my cassock, took the Bible, rosary, and holy water and set out with a brother who was with me for holidays. As we reached the house, the boy began shouting and chasing me out. I invited the Catholic members and others to come together and we prayed in loud voices. I read the scripture passage of Mark 9:14-29 (The Healing of a Boy with a Spirit). The boy fidgeted and screamed. As soon as I finished reading and sprinkling of holy water, the boy grabbed a Manipuri scripted Bible near him, randomly opened the same passage and read aloud. He challenged me saying, "Is it not the same passage you read?" That was wonderful. A possessed Hindu boy opening up a page in that thick Bible and reading to me. Then I believed that even the devil knows the Bible. After that, I cut off the four amulets tight around his waist to ward off the evil eye. He fell down, slept and was better. The following morning, his parents informed me that he was well.

Physical or spiritual healing of a person is initiated as an opposition to the reign of evil and spiritual slavery. If a healer leads the healed and the witnessing community "towards self-understanding and service for others, he is certainly an agent of light" (Israel, 1976, p. 63). On the contrary, if a healer tries to selfishly influence others for personal gain, his gift can indeed assume a demoniac form. In the liturgical life of the Church, there are occasions in pastoral ministry where God's presence and benevolence are honoured, like feasts and festivals.

3.3. Feasts and Festivals

During feasts and festivals, celebrations take the tone of gratitude, remembrance, commitment, challenge to witness. These occasions bring people together and orient them towards the unity of thought, faith and culture. If properly animated, feasts and festivals also consolidate what one believes and perpetuate practice for generations to come.

3.3.1. Commemoration of Saints

The Catholic Church has innumerable saints honoured for their holiness, dedication, martyrdom and valour. Some martyrs sacrificed their lives for Jesus Christ and the Church. These people stand out as persons worthy of imitation. The Catholic Liturgical Calendar provides saints each day of the year for remembrance and imitation. The saints are commonly honoured on "All Saints Day" which falls on 1st November. The commemoration of saints is a clear indication of the relation between the living with the dead. This is a relationship of saints "with us pilgrims on earth and can exercise a power of intercession on our behalf and that of our departed loves ones" (Maloney, 2007, p. 13). The author continues to point out that this belief further gives weight to our doctrinal statement found in "communion of saints, as expressed in the Apostle's Creed" (p. 9). Commemoration of saints manifests "our oneness in love with Jesus Christ, our Head, and His Body, the Church, of which we are His members" (p. 19). Fruitfulness comes when we abide in him (Jn 15:5-12). On June 29, 1943, Pope Pius XII issued the encyclical *Mystici Corporis Christi*, on the Mystical Body of Christ in line with the teaching of St Paul who addresses us as the body of Christ (I Cor 12:27-30) saying, "The Church as a body is frequently asserted in the Sacred Scriptures. 'Christ,' says the Apostle, 'is the Head of the Body of the Church.' If the Church is a body, it must be an unbroken unity" (no. 14). The fact of sharing in one body orients us towards a journey of being united in Christ for a common goal – being Christ-like, a form of perfection. Sherry (1984) points out, "Karl Barth alludes to the list of the fruit of the Spirit given by St. Paul in Galatians V, and says that the limited perfection achieved in this life is the pledge and first fruits of that perfection for which we are destined and which will be manifested when Jesus Christ comes" (p. 1). The metaphor of the body used in the Church is relevant here on earth and life after death.

Invariably, at the time of Baptism, each child is given a saint's name for blessing and protection. Saints become spiritual ancestors or icons for each baptized Catholic. In the words of Sherry (1984) "It is believed that the Holy Spirit makes men like God, that the saints are more like God than ordinary men are" (p. 64). It is an interesting factor to note that even non-Catholics and non-Christians take saints' name as their personal name or institute's name. This is sure, a visible influence of the saints of God. By taking someone's name, one is automatically prompted to imitate or that the person has been influenced already. In this manner, saints' names and ancestors are remembered for good.

3.3.2. Invocation of Ancestors

In the indigenous *Kuki* society, during various rituals, the genealogy of ancestors was chronologically pronounced and remembered to evoke blessings. The Bible, the Christian source of theology, stands as a strong witness to the practice of invoking and remembrance of ancestors. In Genesis 11:10-32, we read a description of "Descendants of Shem." The book of Ezra 8:1-15 records 'Heads of Families who Returned with Ezra' which reads, "These are their family heads, and this is the genealogy of those who went up with me from Babylonia, in the reign of King Artaxerxes…" The Gospel of Matthew archives "The Genealogy of Jesus the Messiah" in chapter 1:1-25. The gospel of Luke 3:23-38 also records "The Ancestors of Jesus." The indigenous *Kuki* phenomenon of calling upon their ancestors make them remember the genealogy tree for posterity.

In the indigenous *Kuki* society, ancestors were considered champions worthy of imitation for their valour and sacrifice. During *Sa-Ai*, a mithun was usually used and "Thempu does the killing after blessing the man who is performing the Sa-Ai after the genealogical tree from *Thadou* has been repeated down to this person" (Shaw, 1929, p. 76). It may sound absurd to a stranger but when you "look at things in the way the believers see them" (Pyysiäinen, 2004, xiii), there is an awe element. In the indigenous *Kuki* society, a child takes the name of his or her ancestors (grandparents or relatives) worthy of remembrance. A peculiar practise of indigenous *Kuki* society is that each person is assigned the last syllable of his or her ancestor to construct a new name. "Kuki names are normally formed of a combination of three to four syllables. This traditional form of naming a child ensures continuity of his or her lineage" (Haokip, 2008, p. 80). Let us take a live instance of my name to clarify this culture of naming. My grandfather's name is *Helkhokhai*. Therefore, I being his first grandson of his only son (Thangngam), my name starts with the last syllable of his name i.e., "Khai." Thus, my name is *Khaikholen*. In this way, my grandfather's name continues through me and many others who have derived their names with the last syllable of his name. In an indigenous *Kuki* society, it is easy to trace the lineage and family of a person. It ensures he or she belongs to a clan and a family. No one can be called an 'orphan' as he or she has derived the name from his or her ancestors.

At rituals for the cure of sickness, and blessings, names of ancestors were invoked to bless the sick and pray for prosperity in new ventures. This may look like ancestral worship to an outsider but it is not worship. Rather, this is regard and respect accorded to ancestors. It serves as a motivation for the younger generation in finding ancestors worthy of admiration. In the Christian tradition, it could be comparable to taking names of saints for emulation and motivation. Just as saints serve as spiritual protagonists worthy of imitation, so also indigenous *Kuki* society projected their ancestors as men and women worthy of respect and imitation.

Given the then scenario where oral tradition was the only means of memorizing, construction of one's name from someone's name perpetuates and forms a powerful means of remembrance and continuity for the generations to come. Shaw (1929) recounts about older folk who tried "to remember the long line of pedigrees and genealogies dated back many, many generations in addition to all the marriage prices, etc., due and to be paid by their line, plus all the feuds" (p. 22). Even cultural songs were never in written format but learnt and memorized by way of repetition. This oral tradition has in some way led the *Kuki* generation to have powerful memories that ultimately led them to compete in the regional and national levels of competitions. Without a doubt, one can conclude that there is a sizable number of officers in Manipur from indigenous *Kuki* society. Undeniably, given their small population of about two lakhs in Manipur, the ratio of *Kuki* officers in the Government sector is considerably high. This phenomenon, we owe to our ancestors for handing down the technique to remembers through repetition of songs, proverbs, idioms, ritual chantings. Therefore, invoking the help of ancestors means a continuation of the same channel of blessing or more.

3.3.3. Success Celebrations

To an indigenous *Kuki* folk, hunting or farming entirely depended on nature and luck, thought to be caused by *Pathen*. Every animal got in hunting, every drop of rain and dew that enhance plant growth are but the exterior signs of the benevolent *Pathen*. Food feasts of success celebrations were the result of *Pathen's* blessing. This prompted them to celebrate with gratitude and offer back to the community what they gained from nature.

Success celebrations could be *Chang Ai, Sa Ai, Chon,* which are signs of magnitude and social responsibility of sharing what one has. *Chang-Ai* was "a very expensive affair which could usually only be done by the wives of chiefs or of very wealthy men" (Shaw, 1929, p. 74). This feast was to be performed three times. The third occasion would be marked by "the *Sheltoldel, Boncho* and *Lholhil* dances… when the person is said to have assured herself a safe entrance and specially selected place at *Mithi Kho*" (Shaw, 1929, 75). Haokip (2008) marks, "Chang-Ai was a feast dedicated to womenfolk's achievement" (p. 82) signifying thanksgiving to God for the fruitful harvest of paddy. It is interesting to note that even shawls signified social status in the indigenous *Kuki* society. Shaw (1929) writes, "Women who have performed this feast are permitted to wear the dark blue cloth with the embroidery at the two ends in red and white cotton of a special design.. The name of the cloth is *Thangnang.*" (p. 75)

The feast of *Sa-Ai* was hosted by men who have hunted ferocious animals. Haokip (2008) remarks, "Sa-Ai denoted a man's wealth, skill and bravery in hunting. A man performing Sa-Ai must have killed many wild and dangerous animals, such as the tiger, bear, elephant and bison" (p. 83). Shaw recounts, "In the old days, only those who have killed all the different kinds of dangerous animals were allowed to perform this ceremony" (1929, p. 75). *Thempu* would appear with *ju* and call upon *Pathen* to permit the "Y-shaped post" (Shaw,

1929, p. 75) to be erected for tying the mithun to be slaughtered for the feast. After some rituals, the animal would be killed and the celebration begins.

This sharing mindset is in direct contrast with the globalized market of commerce and profit where personal wealth accumulation is marked market value. The indigenous *Kuki* success celebrations promoted fellowship, sense of gratitude to God, and above all negated selfish mentality of hoarding things for oneself. The Christian charity of sharing which is a service pleasing to God reminds thus, "Do not neglect to do good and to share what you have, for such sacrifices are pleasing to God" (Heb 3:16). St Luke exhorts us "Give and it will be given to you. A good measure, pressed down, shaken together, running over, will be put into your lap; for the measure you give will be the measure you get back" (6:38).

Those who could perform the feasts of *Chang-Ai* and *Sa-Ai* were thought to enter *Mithi Kho* smoothly and accorded a grand welcome. Therefore, earthly acts were believed to affect life after death. All these acts were ways of sharing their resources got with hard work. It is thought-provoking to note that the indigenous *Kuki* community was already practising basic Christian values even before they officially accepted Christianity as their religion. Therefore, cultural practices can be appreciated and given Christian meaning and respect for effective pastoral ministry.

3.4. Pastoral Commitment of Priests

Catholic teaching says that a priest is "Alter Christus" meaning "Another Christ" (Dunfee, 2009). The author continues to say, this phrase is applied aptly when a priest administers sacraments especially at the celebration of Eucharist, where Christ transforms the ordinary bread and wine into his precious body and blood, through the priest speaking the words of institution. "The essential content of Christ's pastoral charity is his self-gift to the Church and to humanity at large" (Ponnore, 2016, p. 75). This priestly commitment prompts every Catholic priest, allegiance to God and people. This is happy obedience enthused with commitment before God and people.

3.4.1. Commitment Before God

Being a consecrated member of the Church, a Catholic priest's first commitment is to God and the Church. His personal, familial and friendship obligations stand second to the original allegiance he has pledge before God in the sacerdotal ordination. He takes cues from his master, Jesus Christ. At the same time, it would be pertinent to consider the fact that Jesus' whole message was "indebted to a prior tradition of language and thought, an earlier history of faith and prayer" (Auer & Ratzinger, 1988, p. 26). It is evident that the Old Testament was the source of Jesus' message for his audiences. Therefore, Jesus engaged himself in fulfilling the history of faith and prayer as found in the Old Testament. Jesus said, "Do not think that I have come to abolish the law or the prophets; I have come not to abolish but to fulfil" (Matt 5:17). The Catholic priest is also committed in works of the gospel having expressions in varied forms according to the need of time, place and people. Macquarrie (1998) elaborates the regular engagements of a Christian minister in a normal parish set up, thus:

> The Christian minister, whether bishop, priest or deacon, is also a dispenser of the sacraments, or some of them. The typical parish priest baptizes new members of the flock, prepares them for confirmation, celebrates the Eucharist, solemnizes their marriages, visits them in sickness and at the approach of death, eventually buries them and comforts their families and friends. All this pastoral activity requires tack, skill, understanding, sympathy and other qualities. (p. 183)

A Catholic priest is a man for others leaving aside his interests. The people of the parish are his top priority and their concerns are his tasks. A priest should be a person who possesses a loving heart, non-judgemental attitude, forgiving spirit, service-oriented mind, caring heart, one who is Christ-like. The commitment is to remain faithful to God and His commandments. Not only the priest but also the Church being modelled upon Jesus Christ needs to infuse love, forgiveness and care in the world by being intercessor and caretaker. In *Presbyterorum Ordinis*, Paul VI (1965) states:

> Priests, then, can achieve this coordination and unity of life by joining themselves with Christ to acknowledge the will of the Father. For them, this means a complete gift of themselves to the flock committed to them. Hence, as they fulfil the role of the Good Shepherd, in the very exercise of their pastoral charity they will discover a bond of priestly perfection which draws their life and activity to unity and coordination. (no. 14)

Therefore, the faithfulness of God becomes a source of inspiration to serve people more fruitfully.

3.4.2. Intercessor for People

The *Thempu* and Catholic priest actively execute the role of being intercessors to God on behalf of the people. The *Thempu,* chosen amongst the people, is one who has some inclination and affinity towards things of spiritual nature. The Catholic priest, as one "chosen from among mortals, is put in charge of things pertaining to God on their behalf, to offer gifts and sacrifices for sins. He is able to deal gently with the ignorant and wayward since he himself is subject to weakness; and because of this, he must offer sacrifice for his own sins as well as for those of the people. And one does not presume to take this honour but takes it only when called by God, just as Aaron was" (Heb 5:1-4). This is an honoured task of extending God's plan to people in a ministry situation. He must continue the mission of not just transmitting God's word but "must also give account to the Lord" (Podimattam, 2008, p. 28) about his pastoral ministry and present Him the needs and concerns of the people under his pastoral care. Prayer remains a responsibility of the whole Church, pastors, and laity, but the ministers have a particular function by virtue of their calling, a duty of prayer, praise and intercessor (Podimattam, 2008).

In the Old Testament, Abraham interceded before the Lord for the people of Sodom (Gen 18:22-19:29). Moses said to the people, "You have sinned a great sin. But now I will go up to the Lord; perhaps I can make atonement for your sin." So, Moses returned to the Lord and said, "Alas, this people have sinned a great sin; they have made for themselves gods of gold. But now, if you will only forgive their sin – but if not, blot me out of the book that you have written" (Ex 32:30-32). Moses was even ready to die while interceding for his people. Jesus, in the New Testament, died for our sins so that we may have life. Letter to the Hebrews reads, "Consequently he is able for all time to save those who approach God through him since he always lives to make intercession for them" (7:25). Gonsalves (2015) states, "Reality is characterized by the harmonization of the Divine-Human-Cosmic that dynamically interrelate and inseparably engage us in sacramental encounter" (p. 49). As an intercessor, a *Thempu* and a Catholic priest see the interconnectedness of the divine with humans and the cosmic world of births, feasts, festivals, sicknesses and deaths.

The intercessory obligation of a *Thempu* and a Catholic priest extends to life after death. The indigenous *Thempu* was expected to make sure that the dead reach *Mithi Kho* while a Catholic priest is expected to pray for the dead to reach God's abode. In the "New Testament, the phrase 'Kingdom of God,' *basileia tou theou*, or 'Kingdom of Heaven,' *basileia tōn ouranōn*, is the true *leitmotiv* of Jesus' preaching" (Auer & Ratzinger, 1988, p. 24). St. Matthew presents the "Kingdom of Heaven" (Matt 13:44-50) in the parables of treasure hidden, merchant in search of fine pearls, net thrown into the seas. Mark and Luke use "Kingdom of God." The authors continue to remark, "There are in all 122 occurrences of the word in the New Testament, 99 being in the three Synoptic Gospels and 90 on the lips of Jesus himself" (p. 25). The repeated occurrences give an air of special importance in the ministry of Jesus. Auer & Ratzinger (1988) have pointed out the shades of 'Kingdom of God' and 'Kingdom of Heaven', thus:

> The meaning is the same in each case. Behind the Matthaean, usage lies in the Jewish linguistic rule of not using the Name of God, not even the conceptual denomination "God," out of reverence for the greatness of this word. One spoke of him by circumlocution. "Heaven," then is simply a periphrasis of "God." (p. 26)

Conclusion

The indigenous *Thempu* tradition and Catholic priesthood show the value of care for the needy, poor and sick. They foster social relation by way of engagement in the various life situations of people – from birth to death. The pastoral care for sick stands out praiseworthy for imitation and honour.

Signs and symbols used in rituals, prayers, and sacraments speak of the reality of what is incomprehensible to human reason and unseen with naked eyes. To a person who believes in signs and symbols, there is a reality of the signified. Rituals become meaningful when the words, symbols and beliefs go hand-in-hand. They revitalize bond of relation and religious faith.

Saints and ancestors remind us of goodness, valour, holiness, sacrifice and dedication. They have given up their lives for God, a model for us to imitate and be motivated. They are invisible but truly present amongst us in our life's experiences. Therefore, it becomes doubly apt to invoke their names in times of need for valour and healing. Further, we take their names as our personal names to continue their good work.

A Catholic priest and an indigenous *Thempu* are committed to God and people. Their normal day-to-day works circle around people for spiritual or material need. They first owe allegiance to God and then to their personal interests. They are intercessors to God for people, which is a challenging yet honoured vocation. Despite being sinner themselves, they offer sacrifices to God for the pardon of sins and physical wellbeing of people under their care. They have the God-given power to bring grace and blessings upon people. In all ways, they are communitarian people, set apart for religious acts, and serve as sources of inspiration for others. The fourth chapter will present series of face-to-face interviews of people who had immense knowledge about indigenous *Thempu* tradition. The rituals, beliefs and culture are a mine of wealth.

Chapter 4

Methodology, Analysis and Interpretation of Findings

Introduction

The indigenous *Kukis* reside in the area now parts of India, Bangladesh and Myanmar. "The *Thadou Kukis* live in a large area of hilly country bounded by the Angami Nagas of the Naga Hills District in the north, the Province of Burma in the east, the Chin Hills and Lushai Hills in the south and the District of Cachar in the west" (Shaw, 1929, p. 11). The widespread habitation is a phenomenon worth research.

Given here is a selective list of advantages of conducting ethnography quoted by Sangasubana (2011) from a list provided by Wolcott: Ethnography can be conducted entirely by one individual. It is longitudinal, allowing the researcher to observe and record changes over time. It aims at working along with others rather than treating them as mere objects. It allows one to get an insider's view of reality. In this setting, one can gather data in a realistic or naturalistic setting in which people act naturally, focusing on both verbal and nonverbal behaviours of the interviewees.

Therefore, the researcher collected data based on personal experiences of experts in the field of indigenous *Thempu*. This study explored the research topic "Relevance of *Thempu* in Pastoral Ministry" from a socio-theological perspective aimed at effective pastoral management. The interview questions were: Can you describe people's or your understanding of *Thempu*? What were the areas in which the *Thempu* helped people of the village? Can you tell me something about the spirit world? How did the *Thempu* appease spirits? What beliefs do the *Thempu* have about spirits? What were the rituals *Thempu* performed? What roles did the *Thempu* play during ceremonies? What were the things *Thempu* used during rituals? What were the types of animals *Thempu* sacrificed? What training was required to become a *Thempu*? What things were given to *Thempu* as remuneration? What are the similarities and differences between *Thempu* and Catholic priest? What is the relevance of *Thempu* today?

The first part of this chapter deals with research design, setting, selection and sampling description, participants, questionnaire, permission for the research study, data collection tool and method, scope and limitation of the study. The second part, the major portion deals with data analysis and interpretation of findings. This chapter primarily focuses on the various roles of *Thempu* in the indigenous *Kuki* world. From the various personal in-depth interviews, the researcher learnt that the indigenous *Kukis* showed tremendous respect to *Thempu*, which can be evident till today. The *Thempu* did not necessarily prepare medicine but healed people with magical words along with animal-sacrifices that were overt acts to appease spirits. The animal-sacrifices were considered as an exchange for the presumed bonded-spirit of the sick person. When humans were suspected to be imprisoned by malevolent spirits, *Thempu* made clay replicas of mithuns, gongs, cows, pots and others needed items to be offered to spirits in exchange for the spirit of humans.

The researcher tried his best to answer the following overarching research questions:

1. What is the role of *Thempu*?
2. What is the significance of *Thempu* in today's world?
3. What *Thempu* tradition could be integrated into Catholic priesthood?

In many, but indirect ways, research interviewees have answered the research questions. Their experiences were enriching, revealing and provided occasions for socio-theological reflection that could enhance effective pastoral ministry. The experiences gathered serve as tools of knowledge for better interpersonal interaction in ministries.

4.1. Research Design, Setting, Selection and Sampling Description

In this study, the researcher employed the Qualitative Research method trying to elicit first-hand information. The in-depth personal interviews were conducted in different parts of the state of Manipur, India. The research is an ethnographic study of indigenous *Kuki Thempu* as understood by Catholics and non-Catholics – men and women. Reeves (2008) views that "Ethnography is the study of social interactions, behaviours, and perceptions that occur within groups, teams, organizations, and communities." Kuper (2008) gives strong emphasis on exploring the nature of a particular social phenomenon, rather than setting out to test hypotheses about it. Therefore, the researcher tried to extract from different persons, the best of indigenous *Thempu* tradition amongst the *Kukis* of Manipur.

This research used face-to-face personal in-depth interview with a semi-structured questionnaire. The audio interviews in *Thadou-Kuki* dialect have been transcribed into English and coded to deidentify the participants. The coded transcripts have been analyzed using themes to understand the culture of indigenous *Thempu*.

The researcher has been serving as a priest in the Archdiocese of Imphal for ten years and has heard about indigenous *Thempu* tradition. He has seen some indigenous *Thempus* and their roles as well, although many of the original *Thempus* are dead. Therefore, he has chosen this almost extinct form of the indigenous priesthood in the *Kuki* society to throw some light on the younger generation for critical appreciation and meaningful preservation of the age-old good practices.

4.1.1. Participants

The researcher employed purposive sampling technique, chose persons above 50 years of age, at nine (9) different locations of the Archdiocese of Imphal, Manipur, India. They comprised of six Catholics and six non-Catholics, with a woman participant.

4.2. Questionnaire (Appendix A)

The first part of the questionnaire consists of the understanding of indigenous priesthood practised by *Thempus*. They include the general concept and significance of *Thempu* that were prevalent before the indigenous *Kukis* accepted Christianity. Therefore, personal information and personal experiences of individuals were useful. For this, the area of *Thempus'* operation was collected for the fruitful use of information.

The second part of the questionnaire deals with detailed works of indigenous *Thempu* – like how they appeased the spirits, the various rituals performed to ward off evil spirits, the items used for rituals, the types of animals sacrificed, the things given to them, the training required to become a renowned *Thempu*, the similarities and differences between *Thempu* and the Catholic priest. These nine (9) questions were formulated to gather as many details as possible about indigenous *Thempu* tradition.

4.3. Permission for Research Study (Appendix C)

After the approval by Jnana Deepa Vidyapeeth, Ramwadi – 411 014, Pune, Maharashtra, India, permission for this research was obtained from the Archbishop of Imphal, Manipur, India. Permission for the same research was obtained from the participants. They were requested to sign the Consent Form. The participants were assured that no personal, legal, political, economic or any kind of risk was involved in the study as they would remain anonymous. The purpose of the study was explained to them in their mother tongue (Thadou-Kuki dialect). They were informed that this study was in partial fulfilment of the requirement for the Master's Degree in Pastoral Management at Jnana Deepa Vidyapeeth, Pune, India.

4.4. Data collection Tool and Method

The researcher followed the ethnographic Qualitative Research method. The interviewees were selected based on age and expertise in the field of *Thempu* tradition. The data were collected through in-depth personal interviews lasting 60-90 minutes. The questionnaire (Appendix A) was translated into *Thadou-Kuki* dialect (Appendix B) for better comprehension of the interviewees. The researcher himself collected the data while carefully recording the audio question and answers of the participants. The purpose of the project, variables and reasons behind every question was explained to the participants before they made their choice of consent. Majority of the participants signed the consent form themselves. A few who had never held a pen or pencil were helped to complete the Consent Form. The ethics on consent was authentically followed.

4.5. Data Analysis Description

The collected facts were analyzed with the help of ethnographic techniques. The findings were analyzed with appropriate tools, and further elaborately discussed under various themes in this chapter.

4.6. Social Life

The indigenous *Kuki* people were mountain settlers who preferred colder locations than warmer areas. Nature was their only source of sustenance. Their legends, songs, feasts and thought pattern were entwined in and around mountains, rivers, stones, trees, spirits of the forest while they engaged themselves in swidden cultivation. They lived in a small number of families in villages, probably for a better area of cultivation, foliage and hunting. As the younger brother(s) of the reigning chief get matured, they were allowed to leave the village and start a new one. This way of multiplying villages was encouraged and expected in the indigenous *Kuki* society. This phenomenon perpetuated the existence of smaller villages with fewer families even until today. During one of the interviews, GKZ6 has corroborated:

> People lived in mountainous regions. There were no basic needs like – roads, hospitals, transportation, schools, markets, clothing, etc. The only consolation when they get sick was the indigenous *Thempu* who could perform some rituals to heal or prolong life. He was the only hope for survival. Life was a cycle of shifting cultivation, weeding, harvest, some festivals. Some men who had a gun could go

for hunting or those who are good at making traps could get some wild animals as a food supplement.

In their dependence on nature for livelihood, they needed the prayers of the *Thempu* for new land cultivation. Any intrusion into nature needed consultation and ritual, mostly performed by the *Thempu*. JTH12 described this reality in these words:

> The people depended heavily on natural rain and sufficient sunshine. Even to look for new land cultivation, the chief of the village would invite the *Thempu* for prayer and rituals to see if the villagers could cultivate a particular area for a year.

In that given social arrangement, to further strengthen their ties, they had a customary practice of sharing what they gather from nature. "As a sign of respect and allegiance, *Sating* (upper portion of flesh on the spine of a four-legged animal) was given to one's eldest brother and *Sangong* (neck portion of a four-legged animal) was given to maternal grandfather, uncles" (FPH11). In all their daily practices and especially during rituals, "A person should first enter and come out of the house with his right foot" said JTH11. This way of footing was considered a good portent for luck and blessing. Every action undertaken had a meaning and consequence.

4.7. Great Hunt

Hunting was a normal work of an indigenous *Kuki* man. Expert hunters were bestowed social admiration and honour too. JTH3 has confirmed that hunting was a respectable job.

> When a great hunter, after killing a big animal enters the village, he shouts *Kathange* (I am blessed) and shoots in the air to proclaim that he has come with a big hunt. Women of the village would bring their handmade wine called *Vaiju* (fermented rice with husk). He would be served wine and comes home almost drunk. Men of the village would go to welcome him at the entrance of the village gate.

The luck to hunt an animal was a visible manifestation of God's bountiful connection with human beings. The spirits favouring human beings to hunt accentuated the belief in world of spirits prevalent in the indigenous *Kuki* society.

4.8. World of Spirits

Beliefs in spirits and deities were popular. To an indigenous *Kuki*, the spirit of a place or deity of a place signifies the same reality. FPH7 has substantiated this belief when he made his observation:

> Everything around an indigenous *Kuki* was considered to have a spirit. One can cut a tree for use but does not cut a tree without a reason. When someone kills two animals at one shot or at one hunting expedition, instead of becoming happy, he becomes suspicious that some spirits are particularly favouring him. It is believed that one shoots an animal because the spirit who cares for that animal has allowed him to do so. Going to the jungle was also considered a sacred mission with the presumption that the spirits of that area will allow him to shoot an animal. He should not boast or become proud. Rather, with humility, he goes to the jungle for hunting.

The presence of spirits is affirmed by PHH20, when he said, "It is believed that spirits come and join various celebrations of human beings. Spirits were called *Mittungkete* (vertical eyed beings) while humans were called *mitvaikete* (horizontal eyed beings). Spirits were addressed as *Sahem* and humans were addressed as *Mihem*." The earth was thought to be a dwelling place of both *Mihem* and *Sahem*. There was constant social interaction coupled with jealousy between *Mihem* and *Sahem* group of beings. God was thought to be up above in heaven and his influence on earth was tremendous.

4.8.1. Concept of God

Whenever a *Thempu* performed rituals, he invariably called the name of God as *Pathen*. But, JTH10 observed, "the ideas of *Pathen* was there, but the idea of salvation was not in the thought pattern of the indigenous *Kukis*. They believe in a place where the dead will gather, but that is in no way connected to the Christian concept of salvation."

GKZ4 also supported the marred idea of salvation when he said, "The *Thempu*, along with spirits have the power to destroy or build up a household but no power to give salvation to others." They believed in life after death but the idea of salvation was not in the worldview of the indigenous *Kukis*. While *Pathen* was considered the ruler of heaven, they had *Haosa* as their ruler in the village administration.

4.8.2. *Indoi* and White Cock

The sacrifice of a white cock was very special to the indigenous *Kuki* society because their legend says that it was the white cock that made them realize the dawn when they were in total darkness. White cock thus became a symbol of hope, newness and blessing to them. A white cock was sacrificed every year and offered to the household God for further blessings. Important elements of nature, considered to be best in and around them were held together and formed as *Indoi/Doibom*. Further, FPH5 said:

> The best of nature known to *Kukis* were tied together in this symbol of goodness. Doibom was a House God. The elements were like (1) *Vohpi lukon* – the curved skull of a female pig. (2) *Kelchal kikon* – curved horn of he-goat. These signify longevity. (3) *Khaopi thoko nei* – nine-layered bark of a tree used as rope. (4) Miniature basket made of *gomi* – the biggest bamboo in the forest.

PHH22 spelt out some of the ritual prayers pronounced by the *Thempu* while installing the *Doibom*, "*Seupikong nasah bang in nei san, kelchal kikon nasah bang in nei san, vohpi lukon nasah bang in nei san. Neisa sol hih in, neibol sol hih in. Neisah sol, neibol sol le kumtin ju nape pongnge, kumtin sa nape pongnge…* "which may be translated as "Bless me as you bless the basket made of the king of bamboos, bless me to ripe age like a curved horn of he-goat, bless me like a curved mother pig's skull. Do not perturb me. If you disrupt me, I would not offer you the yearly wine and meat."

The practice of installing *Doibom* brought about spiritual and material safety. It signified relatedness to spirit or God. It brought a sense of security, feeling of being guarded by a spirit or God in their own house. CTT25 further stated about *Doibom* and its practice:

> Once a year, a pure white cock, clearly cock-a-doodle-doo, without any blemish was sacrificed for the installation of *Doibom*. This was performed by a family where the husband, wife and children are alive. During April-May, the festival of the sacrifice of a white cock was usually performed. The components of *Indoi/Doibom* were *vohpi lukon, kelchal kikon, gopi tul, khaopi, gomi bom*. The length of the rope would signify life's span; *gopi* was believed to touch the heavens. Goat's horn was to remind them that their forefather Manasseh reared goats as a sign of God's favour. *Si thing*, whose branch had faced the East, was brought home for this ritual's pole. The branch was made to face the East. The feathers of the sacrificial white cock were removed and then the meat boiled without breaking any of its bones. After three days the whole chicken was eaten by the man of the house with *vaiju*. All the bones were stuffed inside the basket made of the king of the bamboos. Another chicken would be prepared for other members of the family.

4.9. Village Administration

The village administration in an indigenous *Kuki* society was conducted by the male progeny of the *Haosa's* family. Daily affairs were executed by the member of the council of ministers. It was an uncomplicated and practical system of administration.

4.9.1. *Haosa*

The indigenous *Kukis* were primarily ruled by self-government under the patronage of *Haosa* and his cabinet. Chieftainship was held by the eldest amongst the brothers, which was further handed down to sons of the eldest brother. JTH6 has confirmed, "The eldest of the brothers should be the ideal chief in the village." In the words of PHH4, "Haosa had to perform the administration of his village just the way the *Thempu* did for the spiritual welfare of the village people."

4.9.2. *Thu Thang*

Every human interaction develops some social or interpersonal problems between themselves. Amongst the indigenous *Kuki* community, problems were there too, and those predicaments were usually settled by the chief and his cabinet with the elders of the village. CTT3 substantiated this trend in his statement, thus:

> In the case of immorality between a man and a woman, the case was handled with utmost secrecy. Only elders above 70 years were selected to decide within closed doors. The news of the unfortunate incident was contained as much as possible. Whatever they decided become the appropriate penalty for the offender. If a young person speaks or hears rumours of immorality, the elders would immediately caution them not to speak about it. They would be warned thus, 'If you laugh at other's fault, it may befall you too.'

This social conduct of mercy was not a sanction for offenders to continue but a chance given to them for improvement without heavy embarrassment before others. Thus, a person had another chance to live and improve.

4.10. *Thempu*

The voluntary post of being an indigenous *Thempu* was held with the highest regard and reverence in the *Kuki* society. He served as a mediator between humans and spirits. He was also considered a healer of sicknesses. He would spend a lot of his time officiating rituals for various persons in his village or other villages. In the observation made by FPH10, there is something unique and praiseworthy of an indigenous *Thempu*:

> The word *Thempu* is unique. It comes from 'Them' meaning 'expert' and 'Pu' means 'originator, owner'. Therefore, it means, the originator of all expertise. This may be so, because, *Thempu* believed that God was the originator of all good. Since he was connected to God in many ways, people might have addressed him as *Thempu*.

During the in-depth interviews, PHH5 confirmed about the respect shown to an indigenous *Kuki Thempu*:

> Mere sight of *Thempu* was a blessing and a sign of health and well-being. *Thempu* would diagnose sicknesses and inform the caretakers of the sick about the need for ritual sacrifices – either mithun, pig, goat, dog, etc. The *Thempu* had to find out the type of spirits to be appeased.

CJK1 was of the opinion that *Thempu* was more of a god-man and a healer. He said, "The *Thempu* did not necessarily prepare medicine but healed people with magical words. He usually made clay replicas of mithuns, gongs, cows, pots for spirits in exchange for the spirits of humans imprisoned by them."

4.10.1. Vocation to Thempu

To be an indigenous *Thempu* was voluntary. It was a tiresome job that demanded integrity, patience, sacrifices and some divine blessings to know the mind of spirits. JTH2 confirmed about the call of the *Thempu* in this words:

> There was no special formal training to be a *Thempu*. Nonetheless, there was always a charisma connected to being a *Thempu*. Deep down in the heart of a person, he should have longing, curiosity, humility and interest to learn from older *Thempus*. The inner desire and learning ultimately groomed him to be a *Thempu*. When a *Thempu* uttered words for rituals, he vaguely uttered to keep that sacredness and secrecy of the chants. Then he would prescribe ways of healing through sacrifice or ritual.

4.10.2. *Themthep* (Remuneration for *Thempu*)

In the indigenous *Kuki* society, the use of money was hardly known. The gesture of gratitude for someone's favour was a social value in practice. The *Thempu* was also rewarded for his time, help and expertise in aiding the villagers. In the words of JTH1, we can find this truth, thus:

> There was hardly any ritual or function done without the involvement of a *Thempu*. Even if he was not able to come for social functions or rituals, he was remembered with *Them sa* and *Them ju*. Every hunter would always remember the *Thempu* of the village when he gets an animal in his hunt.

FPH1 corroborated about the importance and remuneration of a *Thempu*, "A portion of any animal killed especially as part of a ritual was always given to *Thempu* as *Them sa* (meat share of the priest). *Achegu* is the part of four-legged animal given to *Thempu* as *Them sa*. Practically, he had no time to cultivate his own field due to many rituals he had to perform in the village."

4.10.3. Dress Code of *Thempu*

Although, the profession of *Thempu* did not have formal training and declaration as we have in the case of the Catholic priesthood, nonetheless, this vocation was considered sacred. It was considered a difficult vocation. Indigenous *Thempus* also had some uniformity in their way of dressing. PHH1 has this to say, "*Thempu* adorns *tuhsom* – long hair tied up at the top of the head. This was practised by every priest and every matured man of each household." A similar idea was shared by CJK10, thus:

> The indigenous *Thempu* kept long hair, attired with traditional dress. He would not attend ordinary gatherings. He would be invited for big festivities. He wore a kind of 'dhoti' called *Del*, armless shirt called *Boitong* with a turban called *Mangvom*. He wore white *Mangvom* as a turban with a feather of hornbill on happy occasions such as *Chang Ai, Sa Ai, Chon, Hun,* etc. He would don black turban during sad or serious moments like – death, war, epidemics, etc.

4.11. Marriage

Marriage was considered a necessary step to enter into maturity. A man or woman would then be allowed to participate in some of the events where only married people were permitted. In the marriage ceremony, the role of the *Thempu* was indispensable as stated by PHH16:

> The *Thempu* knew about the possible prosperous marriage or misfortune to come. He was like a prophet who could foretell the future. He would pray thus, 'Oh God of our ancestors, I bring to you this couple; they have decided to be together for a lifetime. May you grand them good health with sons and daughters; may they be able to multiply their clan; may they be together until old age and death.'

In a similar tone, CJK16 further commented on the institution of marriage:

> Usually, a young bride was sought from paternal sister's daughters. Sometimes, she was brought to the bridegroom's house with her *kangbom*, meaning her playthings. She does not stay with the prospective husband but cared, trained and looked after by her aunty (would be mother-in-law). Usually, she would be taken during 12, 13 years and kept under the care of aunty for another 3-5 years. She was gradually married off to her prospective bridegroom after her first menstrual experience.

When two matured people agree to marry, the *Thempu* would bless their union as cited by CTT15, performing rituals and prayers:

> During a marriage ceremony, the *Thempu* picks a hair each from the *lujang* (crown of the head) of the bride and bridegroom. The implication was, 'may you both see old age and die.' Two cups of wine were brought in. Inside the two cups, the hair of the bride and groom would be dropped. Then they exchange their cups and drink the wine. The significance of the rituals - from today, we are one head, one heart, one liver. Then, the *Thempu* would hold a cock by the neck to flap its wings as a sign of blessings on the couple. The feather from the back (waist) of the cock was taken and attached to a thread and made into two feather necklaces.

> The *Thempu* would bless them and then garlands the bride and groom as a sign of commitment.

4.11.1. Naming of a Child

If you are an indigenous *Kuki*, it is easy to trace back your lineage because the first syllable of your name is always derived from the last syllable of your immediate ancestor's name. The naming of a person was usually done by elders and not chosen by the child himself or herself. Every naming was a claim and a continuity of the ancestor's name. FPH8 further consolidated the idea of naming and its significance, thus:

> Soon after a child was born, identified as a boy or a girl, a name was proposed immediately by those elders present in the house. This immediate name can be any funny name or anything. The name could be changed later. The belief of immediate naming was that – once a child was born, he or she should be claimed by humans. Though unseen, spirits were also believed to be visiting the human habitat to come and see any newborn child. If not claimed by humans, the spirits around humans would claim for themselves and the child may die soon. Once claimed by humans, he or she was expected to live up to a matured person and die in old age.

In the words of PHH17, "The *Thempu* blesses a new-born child after 2 or 3 days of birth. This was a ritual for longevity and health."

4.11.2. *Lhalho*

Although the indigenous *Kukis* in general and the *Thempu*, in particular, did not have clear articulation about the human soul, they did believe that a soul resides in every human, every animal and created things around them. They would ask God to bless the person and the soul for longevity. CTT18 has confirmed that blessings were sought for the soul through *Lhalho* ritual, usually performed for children, stating thus:

> *Lhalho* was a ritual blessing by a *Thempu* for the soul that resides in the body of a live person. Words like 'may you

> be more blessed than your ancestors' were pronounced. He would drink some *vaiju* and then spinkle just like holy water. *Sa-o* would be tied around the neck of the child as a sign of *Lhalho* or as a sign of being under treatment. Those who had more *sa-o* were considered more sickly than the rest. This necklace was not removed until the *Thempu* declared the sick well.

PHH8 said, *Lhalho* was also performed at the maternal grandparent's house in this manner:

> The grandparents would invite the village priest and request him to bless their grandchildren with the wing flap of a chicken saying – *phe, phe… nang kapi bong cha, kapi kang cha, tunia hi kapet nahi, pu petban, pa petban kapet ahi…* It was done yearly or periodically as a ritual blessing of maternal grandparents and *Pathen*. This kind of ritual paved the way for familial contact and flow of ancestral blessings to the younger generation.

CTT19 has a similar expression about *Lhalho,* thus:

> When a person visits his/her maternal uncle's house, *Lhalho* was usually done for the blessing of the person who was the host's grandchild. A chicken was caught on the neck and made to flap its wings as a sign of blessings upon the person. Then the *Thempu* would read signs from the chicken's legs. If the left leg was the last to move, it was considered a negative omen. But if it happened to be the right leg, it was a sign of posterity, long life and blessing.

4.12. Blessing Rituals

Blessings of the *Thempu* was necessary for most human undertakings. Humans and spirits agreement was desired. Non-agreement was considered unsafe. Mutual respect and consent were the top priority for a peaceful relationship.

4.12.1. New Water Source

A new water source was invariably required before or after starting a new village or before a new swidden field. CTT10 confirmed this tradition of the *Kukis* in this words:

> After they have settled in a new village, they would ask the blessing of God Father and God Mother to ward off spirits from that area so that the site be a blessing of a perennial water source. As a sign of the covenant, they would sacrifice a white cock and consume the cooked meat at the water source.

4.12.2. New Field

Since swidden cultivation was the only option for the indigenous *Kuki* society, they had no other choice but to be in peaceful terms with spirits of the forest. They asked the help of indigenous *Thempu* to divine if that particular area was favourable for cultivation. CTT14 cited some of the prayers performed while looking for a new field, "We are planning to cultivate this land, we are the sons and daughter of Manasseh and God had given us the whole world for our movement. In case you have any objection, kindly let us know." CTT13 said a *Thempu* would perform a ritual to ascertain its favourability, thus:

> *Tuimit san* was performed by a *Thempu* before deciding for a new field. Rice grains were used divining for good or bad omens. Few grains of rice were spread in a small area. After a few minutes, if any grain of rice was found missing, it was a bad omen. If the small area was found with pieces of mud brought by ants, it is a sign that someone would die in this new field. Therefore, it was taken as a bad omen and the plan was aborted for good.

Even after having found a new field to be auspicious, there can be later signs of possible calamity. PHH18 observed that some signs in the field signify misfortune:

> Sometimes, there were strange signs during the burning of swidden field. Example, if people hear strange sounds, shouts, etc., during burning, or a tree uprooted by itself and stands upside down; these were considered some of the signs that owners of the land were unhappy or hurt in the process of burning. Ultimately, the field was abandoned.

4.13. Legend of Hornbill's Feather

In the Northeast of India, many tribal attires and dances spot Hornbill's feather, decked as headgear. For the indigenous *Kuki* people, they have their myth about Hornbill bird and the significance of its feather. This particular lore depicted the plight of being orphaned, cruelty of a foster mother and generosity to share. One of the reasons why indigenous *Kukis* use the Hornbill feather is also derived from this folklore. CJK11 narrated about Hornbill's feather and its rank, thus:

> There was a man with his beloved wife. They had two sons – *Lendou* and his younger brother. After the death of his wife, he married a second wife but she did not love his two sons. She complained about them and asked him to send them away in the forest. The man took a ball of thread along with his two sons and went to a thick forest and left them there. The children came back following the thread laid by their loving father. Even when the young sons came back hungry and tired, the second wife did not show any mercy. Further, the lady covered a live chicken in the mortar (Dhenki/dhinki) at the porch. The chicken pricked her buttock. She made another charge against the two innocent boys and reported to her husband saying 'As I was sitting for my bowel movements in the *Cam*, your boys pricked my buttock. They are naughty. Therefore, send them away.' This surprised their father and he was forced to send them away for eternity.

CJK13 concluded the fable with the significance of Hornbill's feather, stating:

> As they were lost in the forest, *Lendou* climbed up a tall tree to see the direction of their house. He found eggs of Hornbill in a nest. He drank one and dropped an egg for his younger brother too. It broke upon reaching the ground. After drinking a few more eggs, feathers began to grow in his arms and he ultimately became a Hornbill. His younger brother was not able to grow feathers and fly as he had to no chance to consume the whole egg. As *Lendou* was flying around, many people began to ask for his feathers and he began to give them one by one. At last, he was barely able to fly. Therefore, he flew to the house of his younger brother and stayed till new feathers grew. This is the reason every indigenous *Kuki* dons a feather of Hornbill during festivals, dances, and important days. This signifies generosity in giving what one is capable of.

4.14. Important Festivals

The village life would have been monotonous without occasional activities and festivities. Few celebrations associated with agrarian lifestyle were intervals for the indigenous *Kuki* people to relax and unwind their tired physique. PHH15 pointed out an interesting gesture thus, "Before killing a *mithun* for festivals, the *Thempu* would plead the animal to hold no grudge against them. The *Thempu* would pray to spirits that he and the people were to kill this animal for their need, not because of any sadistic motive." In this way, celebrations began with prayer.

4.14.1. *Chavang Kut*

JTH4 pointed out that *Chavang Kut* was one festival that made the indigenous *Kukis* celebrate the bounty of God. It was also a time to meet friends and relax from manual works. The *Thempu* would dedicate the whole village. Merrymaking and drinking of wine was part of the celebration. People prepare wine much ahead of time. They would also prepare *changlhah* – a *Kuki* traditional unleavened bread wrapped with leaves. Young and old would join the festival. Great hunters would be the first ones to drink the festive wine, a sign of honour. There would be sports like long jump, high jump, race, javelin throw, etc. A mithun would be tight to a pole. The ears of the animal would be blocked with ashes, the eyes of the animal were covered with a cloth. The animal would be beaten black and blue over the body. The animals would be tired and almost dead, but still standing. Then men would jump over the animal like a high-jump horizontal pole. As the high jump improves, a *saipikhup* shawl was laid over the back of the animal. If there were still competitors, another *saipikhup* shawl would be added. This feat would be spoken in the village until the next *Chavang Kut*.

4.14.2. *Chang Ai*

The celebration of *Chang Ai* was a voluntary feast hosted by a woman for the rich harvest of paddy in a particular year. This custom encouraged the owner not to hoard up but share by feeding the whole village. It was a thanksgiving gesture and a sign of generosity. CTT20 confirmed of *Chang Ai* feast:

> If a woman had harvested about 1000 *puchas* of paddy, she would celebrate *Chang-Ai* as a sign of gratitude to God. She would offer a feast to the villagers. All the ladies of the village would go to the field of that lady to carry paddy. They would also drop some paddy grains on the way as a sign of abundance. When they return with paddy bags, the lady of the house would be seated at the porch of her house. The *Thempu* would perform *vaiphit* over the head of the seated lady saying 'Today is your day of honour, you are a hard worker, may you be blessed further.'

4.14.3. *Sa Ai*

This particular feast was hosted by a sharp-shooter who has shot many big animals. *Sa Ai* was performed to thank God and also to declare to the village about one's achievements. This ritual was confirmed by CJK17, thus:

> All the heads of the animals the man had hunted would be exhibited at the entrance of his house. A mere number

> of animals was not a sufficient benchmark to celebrate *Sa Ai*. He should have killed animals like Yak, Tiger, Lion, Elephant, Stag, Bear, Hornbill. Skulls or horns of big animals would be exhibited at the top of the house wall and the smaller horns or skulls will be at the bottom.

GKZ1 had similar words of affirmation and description of *Sa Ai,* stating:

> During *Sa Ai*, there was the custom of drinking *vaiju*. Those who had killed animals were seated at the front row with a turban called *Mangvom*. While sipping *vaiju*, those married men who have not killed animals were asked to stand and take the support of a strap as a symbol of shame and defeat. The unmarried, newly married men, were not permissible to partake of that particular wine.

CTT21 further endorsed the reality of this feast, thus:

> *Sa Ai* was performed to thank God. The belief was that when he dies, he will go along with those animals he had killed. When a great hunter was about to die but found difficult to die, the *Thempu* would come and performs a ritual for his speedy and peaceful death saying, 'Gather all the animals you have killed and go peacefully.' Occasionally, some hunters utter, 'I am not able to gather and tame the animals I have killed.'

During *Sa Ai,* Thempu would erect a *Si thing* post in the portico of the celebrant and the latter shouts, *lililili…kathang e, kathang e, salha hung in, vaphol lha hung in, sajuh lha hung in, ngalchang lha hung in, humpi lha hung in, keipi lha hung in, abon a hi tunia kaloupina kasatha nahiuve…* Then, all those gathered men sing *Hanla* – song of bravery. Every man in each house would attend this function.

4.15. Sickness-cure Rituals

Lack of proper medication and diet naturally brought in various kinds of sicknesses and plagues that led the indigenous *Kukis* to depend heavily on the *Thempu*. Therefore, the *Thempu* performed various rituals and sacrifices with an attempt to heal the sick.

4.15.1. *Kithoina*

Different kinds of treatment for sick people were performed. PHH9 said, "When someone was possessed by an evil spirit, *kang gui* was wired in three layers around the house, a dog's open-jaw displayed on the gate-post of the house." Further, this animal sacrifice ritual was recognized by GKZ2, thus:

> Those days, people lived in small houses. Whenever someone was sick, *Khaopi* would be wired around the house as if to fence off the ritual area. A dog was sacrificed and its blood sprinkled around to ward off spirits. The dog was skinned and its open-mount put on a pedestal. A dog's neck was slit and the warm blood mixed with *ai* was given to the sick as a drink. Bamboo sticks were implanted on the ground as a ritual sign. The *Thempu* would perform *vaiphit*. The sick was usually quarantined in a room or corner of the room until he or she was well and hardly anyone was allowed to visit. This practice is called *jechan* – a time of confinement for healing.

4.15.2. Strange Dreams

Along with other various sicknesses, ominous dreams were also considered foreshadowing misfortune. FPH2 confirmed that the *Thempu* was involved in the life affairs of people when they had strange dreams:

> If someone complains of being tied up in a particular spot, the *Thempu,* along with few men would go to that place. They would carry mud-moulds of *sel* and *dah* as gifts for spirits in exchange for the captivated soul. The *Thempu* would catch a *maimom*, lay tread from that spot up to the house as if to bring back the strayed soul of a sick.

4.15.3. Rituals for the Sick

The indigenous *Thempu* was the village doctor. He was consulted and bestowed full authority to treat sicknesses. CTT11 consolidated this claim, stating:

> Every sick person was examined by the *Thempu*. He would feel their pulse and know the type of sickness. He then pronounced if the person was to be treated with a pig, dog, chicken, mithun, etc. Accordingly, the family members and relatives of the sick prepare the ritual sacrifice for healing. For the sake of good health, family members were ready to offer any sacrifice proposed by the *Thempu* even if they were to borrow from others.

The ritual of appeasement done to spirits, with animal-sacrifice for the healing of sickness is consolidated by the words of PHH14:

> When someone was sick, the *Thempu* and some men would go to the jungle, search beneath the leaves and find an insect called *maimom.* It is caught and inserted in a *pumpeng* (hollow reed) covered with cotton. When they happen to cross a river, they would extend the cotton thread from one bank to the other for the spirit of the sick person to climb and find its way. The insect was brought home and released on *godal.* If the person was to live, the insect will go towards the direction of the sick person's bed. If the insect was inactive or chose a different direction, it was considered a bad omen that could invite a disaster of severe sickness or even death.

The treatment of the sick by a competent *Thempu* was further emphasized in the words of CTT24, thus:

> If the person was to be treated by a pig, some pig's hair at the house pillars, beneath the house floor was collected and used for initial rituals. This was called *Tolkhe mul* (fallen hair). The ritual words were like this *'Pusa pasa, nang kagenpinu kagenpipa, tunia hi pu Pathen in nahin sem ahi, longlheng banlheng dinga nahin sem ahi, thikang kisoh hih in,*

> *mankang kisoh hih in, longlheng banlheng ding nahi...* 'A free translation would be, 'You, an animal of my ancestors, today, God has created you, you have been destined to redeem a life. Do not taste death, do not taste defeat, you are to be a scapegoat ...' These words were uttered as if the animal represented by the fallen hair was to be used in exchange for the life of the sick.

In case, the sickness was serious, a bigger animal was required to propitiate spirits. In this kind of ritual, animals became a means to negotiate and redeem the bounded spirits of humans. This belief has been affirmed by PHH6, thus:

> If the diagnosis has been for a big animal like a mithun, the animal was tight in the portico of the house. As part of the initial ritual, a portion of the animal's ear was cut off. It was cooked and used as an initial ritual for the sick. If the result was positive, then the live mithun was tied to a *Si thing.* The *Thempu* would pray, then the mithun pierced with a lance as animal-sacrifice for the wellbeing of the sick. The stomach would be cut open and the sick person asked to enter the stomach thrice as part of the healing ritual.

4.15.4. *Sanenghet*

This ritual was performed to seek blessings from God and ancestors. FPH6 stated, "This ritual was to revive one's relation with God, and continuation of ancestral blessings. This was performed due to a revealing dream of one of the family members or they just decide for *Sanenghet.*" *Thempu* was invited and all the family members were present for this ritual.

4.15.5. *Vum*

Some people knew magical chants to harm and destroy others. *Vum* is spell cast on others. Some hostile occasions prompted individuals to seek the help of these black magic doers. CTT23 spoke about spells cast upon others, thus:

> In one occasion, a charm was cast upon a person. A big piece of animal's skin was soaked in water and made to shrink with magical words. A flying black bee called *khoimi* was employed as a carrier to the target. The targeted person swallowed the small charm while in sleep. After it entered the stomach, it expanded and the target ultimately died. This process could be undone by the sacrifice of a dog. If this was undone by a more powerful *Thempu*, the first doer of charm would be sick and invariably die. Then the truth of his black-magic game would be revealed to others by his ultimate death.

CJK9 affirmed the existence of harmful magic doers thus, "*Thempus* who did black magic or disastrous charms on others got back their share of curses on themselves."

4.16. Death Ceremonies

All those born were finally dead. The process of life was a tough fight with malevolent spirits and sickness. Many ceremonies surround the death of an indigenous *Kuki* member in society. Some rituals of the dead indicate values worth guarding.

4.16.1. *Ahkeng Khai*

Indigenous *Kuki* society was and is still adorned with many customary laws and rituals. Even after death, these rituals and customary laws were faithfully protected. *Ahkeng Khai* was a customary law performed whenever someone died. That was an exterior sign of reconciliation. This practice is continued until today in the indigenous *Kuki* society. The words of JTH9 affirmed the practice of *Ahkeng Khai*, thus:

> When someone dies, *Putes* (maternal uncles) were expected to sacrifice a chicken in the house of the dead as a sign that they have no grudge against the dead person. At times, the chicken's leg is literally hung at one of the house pillars to signify reconciliation. Until this was done, the *Thempu* and others would not discuss about burial or digging of the grave. Death ceremony comes to halt.

Through the observation made by CTT5, it is clear that there were various levels of farewell and burial rituals conferred to different persons. He narrates:

> Grand burial was accorded to chiefs, renowned persons, and those who had a natural death. Grave digging was a tedious job. After the *Ahkeng Khai* ceremony, a pit of about 6 feet deep was dug and then the side of the grave was carved big enough for the entry of the coffin. The respect for the person was that stones or leaves, or mud were not thrown over his or her coffin even after death. A big tree would be fell and a coffin was carved out from that big log. Once a grave was dug, it was not left unattended. Someone had to guard to avoid spirits taking possession of the empty grave.

The presence of unseen spirits in death ceremonies was further affirmed by CTT6 thus, "In case a person comes back to life, the empty tomb was filled with a banana stem to replicate the dead individual. This was a means to placate the spirits as if a dead body has been truly buried."

4.16.2. *Sanglai Tun*

This ritual or custom could be a unique practice unheard off in many other tribal groups. Even after death, the person was still allowed to remain in the house for a few days, to wait for relatives and friends for the final homage to the dead. CTT4 affirmed the custom of *Sanglai Tun*, stating:

> The dead person would be bathed, well dressed and seated on a bamboo basket chair at the main pillar (Sutkhom) of the house called *Sanglai Tun*. The anus of the dead was connected with a hollow bamboo diverted to the outside of the house to let out the liquid from the body. Firewood would be kept at the entrance of the house. The married men relatives of the dead would come to the dead person's house, take a stick, shoot a gun and shout, challenging spirits as to why they have taken the life of their loved one.

The *Thempu* seemed to have a powerful say even to spirits. The role of the *Thempu* for safe passage of the dead was further affirmed by PHH12, thus:

> Just as the dead body was about to be taken out of the house, the *Thempu* would gulp *vaiju* in his mouth and sprinkles around the house saying, 'All you spirits, my elder brother, sister, son or daughter is coming, none of you should disturb his or her way, he or she needs a safe passage.'

The dead were thought to be killed by malevolent spirits. This belief has been substantiated by the words of FPH3:

> Soon after the burial, someone who has not seen the dead on that occasion was usually requested to guard the grave with a gun. Sometimes, a dog or chicken comes to the grave. When shot, it appears to be a lizard or an insect. The dead lizard or animal was thought to be spirits of the evil who have killed that person.

4.16.3. Natural Death Burials

The indigenous *Kukis* consider it a grace to die at old age or die a natural death. In the comments of CTT16, we come to know about how the dead were buried with much respect:

> When a normal person died, the *Thempu* performed some rituals. At the veranda, he would summon some men to stand in two rows in odd numbers like five each or seven each on either side. Then he takes a cock and utter words like this: *Agilsahlou nadu am? … lililili…..* Then, men of each row respond by hitting the firewood on the wooden floor. They do this for 3-5 times. Then the dead was taken down from the basket cage and placed in the coffin and brought out of the house. Over the grave, some food items like rice, seasoned wine in a traditional gourd were served for the dead to feed on. *Kep* was a pole erected on a man's grave. On it, some sticks or bamboos were placed horizontally to count the number of big animals he killed during his

> lifetime. Animals like deer, chimpanzee, monkey, etc., were not counted as big hunt. Therefore, the horizontally placed sticks meant animals like tiger, lion, bear, yak, stag, elephant, etc. The dead were usually buried in the portico of the house. Burial in the portico was also a way of marking one's residence or territory of that particular person and descendants.

A similar burial accord, though of a lesser degree, was given to women. CTT17 descriptively notes with these words:

> When a woman died, nothing great was done unless she belonged to the chief's family. An inquiry would be done whether she has been *akilha,* which means the traditional farewell from her family after her marriage. If proper traditional farewell had not been accorded her, an animal would be slaughtered by her family members and a meeting with the husband's family would be conducted. The latter would be asked about the bride price paid and how much still to be paid. Accordingly, death ritual followed when her *man* (bride price) has been amicably agreed upon.

4.16.4. Accidental Death Burials

To die an unnatural death was considered a curse for the victim and family members. The accidental dead persons were not even brought inside the village. They were shown burial ground outside the village. This practice was affirmed by the words of CTT1, thus:

> If someone was killed by an animal, she or he was buried outside the village. If she or he was shot by another man or killed by another human person, she or he will be buried across the river of the village to make sure that the spirit does not come to the village. It was thought that spirits cannot cross a river and ultimately they would lose the direction to the village. This was done to prevent further unwelcome accidents of this sort happen in the lives of the villagers.

To confirm that unnatural death was a curse, we have CTT2 and his words:

> Curses like "*Kho veilam a nalup, kho jetlam a nalup*" means "May you lay on the left side of the village, may you lay on the right side of the village." This was one of the peak curses one could expect. Those who met unnatural death were accorded the left or right side of the village as a burial ground. In any case, the dead were laid to rest for the satisfaction of the relatives.

4.16.5. Place of Meeting After Death

In the indigenous *Kuki* society, death was considered a moment of corporal separation. After death, they spoke about a place of stay call *Mithi Kho* (village of the dead). The concept of *Mithi Kho* is not very clear until today. There are no concrete examples to cite and argue for its authenticity. But, they believe that a place of this sort exists where the dead stay after earthly existence.

PHH11 opined, "At *Mithi Kho*, *Khulsamnu* would disturb women, children and ordinary people with her personal works. Great chiefs, great hunters who have killed big animals were respected by *Khulsamnu*. She would give an undisturbed passage to them."

The belief in the existence of the soul was affirmed by the practice of asking the dead person's soul to come out of the grave. PHH13 affirmed this belief, thus:

> A *Nangjang* was inserted into the empty tomb as if to call out the soul of the dead to avoid being buried with the body. The *Thempu* would bless the empty tomb with *vaiphit* and say 'May the spirit of my brother, sister, father, mother, uncle, aunty son, daughter come out.'

Conclusion

The comment of JTH7 is worth a quote, "With the coming of Christian missionaries and condemnation of indigenous *Kuki* practices, we lost much traditional wisdom. There is alienation from indigenous *Kuki* roots, cultural practices; even abhorrence of the olden day's practices of our ancestors." Going back to the sources of one's cultural roots is an accurate exercise of getting more insights to begin a people-oriented theology for practical and effective pastoral ministry. Reflection in ministry should begin from the wisdom of the past and prudence to deal with contemporary contexts.

The appreciation of one's culture is an appreciation of the variety God has endowed our ancestors. Indigenous culture existed before formal religion. Therefore, one cannot completely ignore one's cultural roots at the acceptance of formal religion. Cultural heritage with its richness and depth can work well with Christian religion which also has sprung from a conglomeration of Judeo-Hellenistic culture.

The concept of leadership should be viewed in the light of selfless service to the needy and poor. Not fossilizing the older practices of the indigenous *Kukis*, but accelerating the dynamics with today's contextual phenomena can pave ways for mutual acceptance, sharing and enrichment. The various rituals for the sick, the dead and belief in the existence of the soul have an indigenous origin. These practices can be given gospel value in the Catholic priesthood tradition.

A path of mutual enrichment, rather than alienation from one's culture is an important aspect of theologizing in the indigenous *Kuki* society. A contextualized Catholicism can be a guiding star, a home for many and a garden of variety. Then, one can theologize and find the relevance of indigenous *Thempu* culture for pastoral ministry that is historical and contextual.

Chapter 5

Discussion for Pastoral Implications

Introduction

Methodology, analysis and interpretation of findings in Chapter IV has revealed that the concept of God was not very clear to indigenous *Kukis* in general and *Thempus* in particular. Nevertheless, they used words like *Pathennu, Pathenpa* (God Mother, God Father) while addressing spirits in rituals. Use of magical words seemed to have originated from legendary heroes like *Galngam* and *Hangsai*. In today's Catholic Christian context, *Galngam* and *Hangsai* could be considered patron saints of indigenous *Kuki Thempus*. From birth to death, the role of the *Thempu* was significant. The belief in the words of Jesus held with great conviction in Catholic priesthood go congruent with the belief in ritualistic words pronounced by indigenous *Thempu* in the *Kuki* society.

It is a clear phenomenon that in Christianity, topics such as Christology, Ecclesiology, the Trinity, Ecumenism, Interreligious dialogues and God are ever ongoing topics of discussion. So, it would be wiser to think "theology as the actual process of quest and reflection in the ongoing life of believers rather than as a single set of answers" (Davies, 2008, p. 2). In this chapter, this quest and reflection will lead us to identify God in the *Thempu* tradition under various headings such as Indigenous Priesthood, Respect for Human life, Indigenous Ecological Care, Sharing as Detachment, Respect for Women, Spirit of Forgiveness, Death, Hope for Life beyond Death and Indigenous *Kuki* Eschatology.

Just as any scientific research favours interdisciplinary outlook, it is not possible to explain one indigenous *Kuki* ritual as a watertight compartment without relating to the others. The fact is, all rituals are related to each other, and explanation of one or few will be insufficient to know the whole portrait. A holistic idea of all the rituals will serve as a good platform for a further imprint.

5.1. Major Research Findings

The major findings of this ethnography and ethnohistory research have revealed a wealth of indigenous *Kuki* traditions in matters about their relationship with spirits, among themselves, with nature and their hope for the future. The findings serve as values for imitation and themes for further deliberation.

5.1.1. Indigenous Priesthood

Although, being *Thempu* had no fixed and fat remuneration, his call was directed towards the welfare of others. Therefore, he went on doing service for the villagers. Without being consciously aware, the *Thempu* had practised this biblical passage of "Whatever your task, put yourselves into it, as done for the Lord and not for your masters, since you know that from the Lord you will receive the inheritance as your reward" (Col 3:23-24). The various roles he played in the village affairs were praiseworthy. He worked in collaboration with the chief, the head of the local self-government of that time. The general conception among the present generation *Kukis* about indigenous *Thempu* is that he was a pagan icon, busy with mystical words, used unknown chantings, and a worshipper of the devil. Therefore, he was an opposition to the concept of God presented by western Christianity. This misplaced concept could be due to dearth of in-depth knowledge about one's traditional roots, added by blind adherence to something foreign. After the in-depth personal interviews, the researcher found that the indigenous *Thempu* was deeply religious, committed to serving the villagers and concerned about the soul and physical health of the people.

The indigenous *Kuki* priesthood popularly known as *Thempu* had profound regard in the *Kuki* society. Although, the *Thempu* was not necessarily the most educated or gifted person of the village, he had the respect for being a person close to *Pathen* and spirits. The *Thempu* was invariably associated with rituals in his dealings with people in the village. As an image of God, the *Thempu* was a source of hope for the sick, a knowledgeable person in divination to know the mind of spirits in various rituals and events of a village community. He was a man consciously involved in safeguarding human life at all cost. He was present at the birth of a child, during sickness, death and even at the customary rituals for the soul after death. He represented people before God as intercessor especially during the time of sickness and plagues.

The *Thempu* was an image of blessing. His presence and mere sight invoked blessings. He was a personification of hard work, sacrifice, patience and dedication in the village. His keenness to serve others usually delayed his plantation of crops, timely weeding which ultimately forfeited him from fruitful gathering from the field. He had a powerful memory to recite long ancestry of clans, people and the multitude ritual chantings. His association with God, spirits and the civil village head - *Haosa* was a good example of co-existence and diplomacy at its height. He represents a healthy coexistence of secular and religious sectors in a community.

5.1.2. *Indoi/Doibom*

The indigenous *Kuki* society considered *Indoi/Doibom*, made of the best articles of God's creation. This makes sense because God was considered best and perfect. Therefore, the best of nature represented God's presence and power. The indigenous *Kuki* people's religious adherence seemed to centre around *Indoi/Doibom* – the source of blessing for every household. The *Thempu* was a connecting factor to consult, appease and remind the people about the anger of spirits, mind of spirits and *Pathen* (God) present in nature. From faith's perspective, *Indoi* was a sign of God's physical presence and a reminder to the family for good conduct worthy of being God's children.

Natural elements bound together in *Doibom* was a mixture of "flora and fauna" (Chongloi, 2008, ixx). The symbolic depiction of *Pathen* was for fertility, birth and continuance of generation. The opposite condition of being infertile was considered a curse in some way. The symbol of *Indoi*, in a way, fructifies marriage or was expected to fructify it. Shaw (1929) has recorded that during the installation of *Indoi*, the *Thempu* prayed to *Pathen* so that "the householder may have many sons and daughter, riches and power and a long life" (p. 74). Rather than merely being stuck to the symbol of *Indoi,* one should carefully perceive what the symbol symbolizes. If the book of Genesis was considered to record "the fall" of humanity and the doctrine of "original sin" (Greenberg, 2018, p. 8), which means separation from God, *Indoi* could be viewed as a symbol of God's presence. If the Genesis story of God interacting with human became the basis of fall, then the interaction of God with humans in the *Indoi* symbol becomes *Kukis'* first instance of obedience and allegiance to God. If the sin of disobedience from the part of Adam and Eve (Gen 3:1-24) have in some way tainted the rest of human beings, the institution of *Indoi* can be viewed as a sign of obedience to God revealed to *Kimchal* (Shaw, 1929). The first purpose of installation of *Indoi* was for *Kimchal* to beget children after the loss of his daughter *Japhal.*

5.1.3. Spirit of Forgiveness

Particularly, through the indigenous *Kuki* cultural practices of *Ahkeng Khai* and treatment of *Thu Thang,* one can conclude the general practice of forgiveness, a Christian core value. Forgiveness was extended during a lifetime and even after death. The indigenous *Kuki* practice of *Ahkeng Khai* by maternal uncles is a powerful sign of reconciliation. This foreshadows the belief of meeting in *Mithi Kho,* which is a remote form of *Kuki* eschatology that needs further investigation.

In cases of unfaithfulness (adultery, sexual offences), the man was cornered by the elders in a closed room. This kind of news was called *Thu thang/Thu Se* which means "bad news, unwanted news, dirty news." CTT3 substantiated this trend in his statement, "In case of immorality between a man and a woman, the case was handled with utmost secrecy. Elders were selected to decide within closed doors. The news of the unfortunate incident was restricted as much as possible." Village elders decided matters regarding the offence and penalty to be imposed. Then, reconciliation was initiated between the parties through a fellowship meal. The meat from this fellowship meal was shared by the elders of the village. The young unmarried men and women, young married people were forbidden to partake of this meal, lest this kind of misfortune befalls them. No one was permitted to talk about this particular issue in the village. In this indigenous manner, offenders were given a second chance to become better persons in life. It was not a formula for offenders to go scot-free. This is forgiveness – a Christian value found practised in the indigenous pre-Christian *Kuki* society even before accepting Jesus Christ as God. Peter's question to Jesus, "Lord, if another member of the church sins against me, how often should I forgive? As many as seven times?" Jesus said to him, "Not seven times, but I tell you, seventy-seven times" (Matthew 18:21-22) can still be a relevant virtue. Jesus proposes unlimited forgiveness. Humans are limited beings and most of the time they have limited patience and forgiving spirit.

The customary law of *Ahkeng Khai* was performed whenever someone died as an exterior sign of reconciliation. The belief that they would meet again prompted them to forgive each other if not during a lifetime, at least at death. Some of the pre-Christian indigenous cultures followed by the *Kuki* society under the patronage of the *Thempu* were very Christian in essence. The *Kuki* society was and is adorned with many customary laws and rituals until today. Even after death, these rituals and customary laws are still faithfully conducted.

Indigenous *Kuki* belief of animal-sacrifice implied shedding of blood as expiation for the offence caused to spirits and a means of reconciliation. The animal-sacrifice ritual was to bring about healing to the soul and body of the sick. Therefore, when Christianity came in contact with the indigenous *Kuki* society in the later part of nineteen century, the missionaries preached about Jesus Christ who died for the sins of human beings by shedding his blood and giving up his life. This message was accepted by indigenous *Kukis* because they already had a similar kind of thought pattern in the rituals so far performed by the *Thempus.* The Biblical narratives of Jesus crucified, that involved shedding of blood was taken well by the indigenous *Kuki* society. The Catholic belief of 'The institution of the Lord's Supper' became a message that augmented their belief of sacrifice of blood to spirits for the soul and body of a person. Matthew, the evangelist records, "When they were eating, Jesus took a loaf of bread, and after blessing it he broke it, gave it to the disciples, and said, "Take, eat; this is my body," Then he took a cup, and after giving thanks he gave it to them, saying, "Drink from it, all of you; for this is my blood of the covenant, which is poured out for many for the forgiveness of sins" (Matt 2:26-28). The indigenous *Kukis* believed in the words of *Thempu,* so also the words spoken to them by a Catholic priest who represents God in some way. Catholic priests who are specially ordained to continue the Eucharistic celebration is an appealing symbol that has replaced the indigenous *Thempu* who was involved in a blood sacrifice for the welfare of people. It may not be an exaggeration to say that rudiment of beliefs in Eucharist was already existent in crude form in the indigenous *Kuki* society before Christianity came in. Therefore, Catholic priests are very much respected in the *Kuki* society. Similar respect is shown to pastors, evangelists, preachers, in other denominational churches amongst the *Kukis.* The indigenous *Kuki* belief of animal-sacrifice (blood and flesh), performed by the *Thempu* in exchange for the thought-to-be imprisoned soul of the sick creates a large avenue to reflect and theologize.

5.1.4. A Future Place for the Dead

In the indigenous *Kuki* society, death was considered a moment of physical parting from the community. After death, they spoke about a place of stay call *Mithi Kho. Mithi Kho* was believed to be a place for dead people. This ultimately offers a ray of hope for life after death that earthly deeds have repercussions in life after death. Reconciliation and forgiveness were considered necessary to get a place in *Mithi Kho.* That is the reason, the ritual of *Ahkeng Khai* was insisted upon. *Thempu* was a necessary agent to pray for the dead person and facilitate entry of the soul to *Mithi Kho*. At death, the *Thempu* performed rituals without any discrimination against gender or clans. His role as an intercessor was significant and highly appreciated.

To write about death, a mysterious phenomenon on earth when I myself have not experienced may sound unreal. However, as a Catholic priest, I have seen and been around various kinds of deaths, and it is meaningful to see death from a theological perspective. The indigenous way of respect shown to the dead, rituals performed after death, the belief of meeting again in *Mithi Kho* can very well be elucidated in the Christian theology of death. Evasion of the theme of death, judgement and afterlife could keep us in darkness. Garvey (2005) says, "Avoidance of these questions not only keep us from leading fuller, more profound and even joyful lives but neglecting them can spoil our days and our relationships with other people" (p. 2). In the indigenous *Kuki* society, mourning the dead went on for days, perhaps, a sign of honour and chance given to relatives and friends to come from other villages to perform their customary practices. The Bible has passages of death mournings: "When all the congregation saw that Aaron had died, all the house of Israel mourned for Aaron thirty days" (Num 20:29), "The Israelites wept for Moses in the plains of Moab thirty days; then the period of mourning for Moses was ended" (Deut 34:8).

The above themes about indigenous *Kuki* culture and the Catholic Church could enlighten and serve as a launching pad for deeper theological reflection. In that sense, "Theology of Death in indigenous *Kuki* society" could be another interesting discussion. The researcher is not engrossed in the reality *per se* about life beyond death but tries to expound the belief in life after death that was firmly held in the indigenous *Kuki* society. The customary practice of *Ahkeng Khai* that symbolizes forgiveness, farewell and expectation to meet in *Mithi Kho* are entwined indigenous practices found in the *Kuki* society. In *Evangelium Vitae* (1995), Paul II stated, "The Gospel of life, proclaimed in the beginning when man was created in the image of God for a destiny of full and perfect life (Gen 2:7; Wis 9:2-3), is contradicted by the painful experience of death which enters the world and casts its shadow of meaninglessness over man's entire existence" (no. 7). Death, in some way projects itself as a limit, a boundary from which no physical human can continue to live.

The melancholic nature of death usually debars humans to dwell into a discussion. The theme of 'Death' could bring in fear, anger, separation, anxiety, uncertainty, depression. Indigenous *Kuki* theology of death could be described as the victory of malevolent spirits over the human spirit. Catholicism sees death from another angle, as a cause of sin. St. Paul states, "For the wages of sin is death, but the free gift of God is eternal life in Christ Jesus our Lord" (Rom 6:23). St. Paul continues to assert, "Therefore, just as sin came into the world through one man, and death came through sin, and so death spread to all because all have sinned" (Rom 5:12). Displeasure, hurt or turf invasion of spirits by way of cutting trees for cultivation could be considered sins against spirits that caused sickness to the body and soul of human beings. "Much Christian writing and preaching about death implicitly denigrated the body and the flesh" (Garvey, 2005, p. 70) almost suggesting the spirit superior to the flesh. However, in the indigenous *Kuki* society, the health of the body was needed for the health of the soul too. Garvey (2005) shares his parish experiences when dealing with death experience:

> Where death and the afterlife are concerned, most Christians are functionally Neoplatonists. Neoplatonism influenced many early Christian thinkers, Augustine among them. They found the soul not only superior to the body, and an entity quite separate from the body, but they considered the body an encumbrance, something we will be happy to escape (p. 70).

The concept of *Mithi Kho* is not very clear whether that was the final place of the dead or another place existed after that. There are less tangible examples to cite and argue for its validity. The fact is, they believe about it. Those who have killed animals or harvested plenty of paddy and fed the villagers through *Sa Ai, Chang Ai,* etc., were thought to be given an honoured place in the village of the dead (Shaw, 1929). Good deeds performed on earth was believed to have an effect in life beyond death. The last rituals performed for the dead became first rituals for his or her entry into *Mithi Kho*. Death became a shift from being a citizen of a village to attain citizenship of *Mithi Kho*. The food offered on the grave became the first meal for his or her journey to the next life. Life was transformed, not completely ended. Even the spirit of the dead was thought to be lingering around the house for a few days. The hope of meeting at *Mithi Kho* serves as a motivation to forgive others. This firm belief in *Mithi Kho* and hopeful expectation to meet again paves the way for indigenous *Kuki* eschatology at its infantile stage.

5.1.5. Christian and Indigenous *Kuki* Eschatology

Indigenous *Kuki* eschatology is an area for finer theological reflections. The indigenous *Kuki* eschatology rises from belief in *Mithi Kho*. There are no concretely approved and available written materials on this. If other indigenous *Kuki* rituals were orally transmitted, then the oral tradition of belief in *Mithi Kho* also stands valid for those who believe. With the coming of western Christianity that spoke on judgement and life after death, the concept of sin, good deeds and bad deeds have become points for theological discussion in the indigenous *Kuki* society.

This section does not attempt to present an exhaustive narration of Christian eschatology but tries to highlight some basic beliefs of eschatology as signposts for the discussion to go on. The hope of life after death connects life here on earth and life beyond earthly existence. It casts a ray of hope and a sense of responsibility to the living. Pitching on basic Christian eschatology, the indigenous *Kuki* eschatology can be evaluated. On the other hand, one could also argue that indigenous *Kukis* could look at Christian eschatology from the perspective of their own cultural hint of eschatology. To limit Christianity without eschatology would be an unfinished task. Braaten & Jenson (2002) opine, “Contemporary people can no longer share the eschatological beliefs of the first Christians” (p. vii), which could be due to cultural alteration, modern belief and lack of faith in Jesus. The authors further state, “The futurist images and beliefs that the early Christians inherited from Jewish apocalypticism were classified as mythical, and thus has so much husk that the winds of time have swept away” (p. viii). The present secularistic mindset has added to considering eschatological concepts a mythical topic for discussion. At the most, one can think of life after death as much as we experience life here and now or take the support of 'hope' to think of unseen, unheard and not yet experienced life beyond death. St. Paul reminds the Romans, "May the God of hope fill you with all joy and peace in believing, so that you may abound in hope by the power of the Holy Spirit" (15:13). From a Christian theological view, death means meeting God face to face for the final judgment followed by reward or punishment (Matt 25:31-46). It is possible, "we console ourselves with images of an afterlife, considered often as if death meant only a change of scenery or condition" (Garvey, 2005, p. 2). Proper theology of death can be viewed from the theology of life itself. Life serves as a means to death; death, a means to a new life promised by Jesus, "Truly I tell you, today you will be with me in Paradise" (Lk 23:42).

5.2. Germane Tools for Pastoral Management

After deep reflection coupled with a decadal experience of priestly ministry in various pastoral settings, the researcher is prompted to recommend some germane tools for effective pastoral ministry. Though not exhaustive, these suggestions could serve as cursors for further sharpening and development of themes for discussion.

5.2.1. Respect for Human Life

The indigenous *Kuki* cultural practice of *Lhalho* or *Lhakou, Sa-o, Sanenghet, sanglai tun,* rituals at the death of someone signified the importance of human life and respect accorded to it. Cultic ritual prayers for children discussed painstakingly in Chapter III reminds a pastor about the sanctity of life. Those moments were occasions to acknowledge God's love in the form of birth. The *Thempu* and the people who rejoiced and appreciated those occasions represented a community support system ready to help out in good times and lean seasons of life. In *Donum Vitae* (1987), in the introduction to 'Teaching of the Magisterium', John Paul II, stressed on the sacred nature of life saying, "Human life is sacred because, from its beginning, it involves 'the creative action of God' and it remains forever in a special relationship with the Creator, who is its sole end. God alone is the Lord of life from its beginning until its end: no one can, in any circumstance, claims for himself the right to destroy directly an innocent human being" (no. 18, 19). The indigenous *Kuki* culture of safeguarding life in the womb of a woman, celebration at birth and rituals for health and wellbeing were Christian in nature originating in a non-Christian environment. The ritual practices of *Lhakou* as mentioned in Chapter II under the heading "Indoi or Doibom" was a sign of respect to human life.

Any child born in the family was respected and accepted as the greatest gift of God. Naming a child was not an individual affair but discussed by the child's grandparents and relatives to arrive at a meaningful name. The indigenous *Kuki* practice of deriving name from the last syllable of his or her ancestors continues family lineage forever. Begetting children and having many children was considered a sign of God's favour amongst the indigenous *Kukis* then and even now in this Christian era. Because of this understanding, the rituals for pregnant women, ritual at birth, *lhalho, lhakou* (Haokip, 2000) became prominent rituals for celebration and get together.

The fifth commandment, "Thou shall not kill" portrays the sacredness of life. The irreplaceable nature of human life prompts us to respect life in all forms. Keenan (2005), writing on "Suffering, the Body and Christianity" said, "human life is singular; that it is created in God's image; that it is uniquely created by God for a special relationship with God… and that finally is, in turn, the source and end of human life" (p. 54). People celebrating the birth of a child in the indigenous *Kuki* culture initiated the aimed-relationship with God.

The respect shown at birth continues in illness-treatments when one gets sick. Human suffering was respected and the freedom to request for aid (Keenan, 2005) was powerfully seen in seeking help from the *Thempu* by way of rituals for good health. The sick were free to express their sufferings with a high chance of being attended too. Freedom of expression was a value. Their livestock such as mithuns, dogs, pigs, fowls, etc., were their life-insurance agencies. Care for the body corresponds with the scriptural regard of the body as "the temple of the Holy Spirit" (1 Cor 6:19). Keenan (2005) further marks, "The body is central for understanding Christianity.

Through the body, we understand God, our worship, our destiny, and our communal identity" (p. 54). It becomes meaningful to be bodily present for liturgical worship and other human gatherings. The incarnation of Christ as a human person with body and soul becomes a message acceptable to indigenous *Kuki* society. It becomes meaningful to hear that God loved us and gave his only son (Jn 3:16) to interact and teach us the way to the Father. This accords weight to the feeling of loss when one is not bodily present or has died.

The Christian initiation of Baptism serves as a symbol of one's insertion and acceptance into the human community of faith. It can be rightly said that this is a "celebration of faith and hope in the community of salvation in Christ. We experience in baptism our personal insertion into the new and eternal covenant, as members of the chosen people" (Haring, 1976, p. 139). Sin, as considered by Christians came into humanity, ultimately causing death. Initiation of this sort is a symbolic cleansing of human sins in order to find favour in the side of God. For "if we say that we have no sins, we deceive ourselves, and the truth is not in us" (1 Jn 1:8). Baptism, as a sacrament, initiates us to live Christ-like.

Therefore, the indigenous *Kuki* culture of respecting human life from before birth, after birth and the rituals for the dead are meaningfully situated in the Christian theology of the body. The achievement of a person while alive (with a body) was considered needed for his or her entry into the afterlife dwelling (Mithi Kho), where good deeds like Chang *Ai, Sa Ai*, etc., were considered worthy of appreciation. St. Paul proudly proclaims, "Christ will be exalted now as always in my body, whether by life or by death" (Phil 1:20). The assurance that Christ can be glorified in our body while we are alive gives us the worthiness to be counted as part of Christ. Catholic theology gives a privileged place to the 'body' in the belief of the incarnation of God in Christ (Lk 1:31); the celebration of Eucharist where Catholic Christians partake of the body and blood of Christ (Jn 6:53-56); the belief in the resurrection of the body (I Cor 15:35-58); and the Church, fondly addressed as the body of Christ (Keenan, 2005). Admitting God's generous gift of nature for sustenance, indigenous *Kuki* society gave high respect to every animate and inanimate thing in their surroundings that prompted them for ecological care.

5.2.2. Sharing as Detachment

The earth is our common home, we are visitors on this earth and no one is a permanent dweller here. We were born empty and we cannot carry any material things after death. The indigenous *Kuki* society entirely depended on nature and whatever harvested from nature was considered a gift to be shared. The cultural practices of bountiful paddy harvest feast as *Chang-Ai,* a great hunt feast as *Sa-Ai* discussed exhaustively in Chapter III were tangible occasions to be grateful to God by way of sharing one's wealth, harvest, luck and blessings with community members.

Chang-Ai was "a very expensive affair which could usually only be done by the wives of chiefs or of very wealthy men" (Shaw, 1929, p. 74). *Chang-Ai* was a voluntary feast hosted by a woman for the rich harvest of paddy in a particular year. This encouraged the owner of the paddy not to hoard up but share with the community by feeding the whole village. It was a thanksgiving gesture and a sign of generosity and detachment. CTT20 confirmed of *Chang-Ai* feast stating, "If a woman has harvested about 1000 baskets of paddy, she will celebrate *Chang-Ai* as a sign of gratitude to God and offer a feast to the villagers."

Sa-Ai feast was conducted by a great hunter who has killed many big and ferocious animals of repute. "In the old days, only those who have killed all the different kinds of dangerous animals were allowed to perform this ceremony" (Shaw, 1929, p. 75). This feast was performed to thank God and also to declare to the village about his valour, luck, blessings and achievements as a hunter. This ritual was confirmed by the words of CJK17, "The heads of animals hunted would be exhibited at the entrance of his house. Heads of big and small animals would be exposed at the top and bottom of the house wall."

The spirituality of feeding others is that nothing permanently belongs to an individual. A good hunter hunts to feed neighbours; a hard worker in the paddy field harvests for those around her. The success celebrations discussed in Chapter III are signs of God's bountiful blessings either on a woman or man which is culturally and visible celebrated as *Chang-Ai* and *Sa-Ai* feasts. Further, these good works were believed to merit them respect in life after death at *Mithi Kho* (Shaw, 1929). The biblical exhortation, "Do not neglect to do good and to share what you have" (Heb 3:16) was already in the practical state. The Christian ethics of non-attachment, the spirit of sharing and of awareness of being pilgrims on this earth were clearly honoured in these indigenous *Kuki* practices.

The indigenous *Kuki* practice of sharing one's property in the form of feasts stands in sharp contrast to the present mindset of being rich through one's personal hard work. The indigenous values set against the present economic values confuse the minds of people. The then indigenous *Kuki* society considered abundance as a pure sign of unmerited God's blessing meant to be shared. The same indigenous *Kuki* society, after beings Christians, considers wealth as a sign of one's personal productiveness. Today, even property gained from unfair means are considered as God's blessing provided one gives tithe or donations to spiritually related activities. This is placating God with mammon which the researcher thinks, is unchristian at its core.

5.2.3. Respect for Women

One of the most important reasons for installing *Indoi/Doibom* was to acquire the blessings of God by way of begetting children. Needless to say, to be barren was considered a curse. Therefore, a child born, whether male or female was considered a blessing happily received without grumbling. In the indigenous *Kuki* society, a girl or woman has been respected from the moment of birth. The indigenous *Kuki* cultural practice of *Lhakou* or *Lhalho* were performed for a male and female child without an iota of distinction. Every sick child was attended to.

"Chang-Ai was a feast dedicated to womenfolk's achievement. It was celebrated as a thanksgiving for a bounteous harvest, the fruit of their labour" (Haokip, 2008, p. 82). The indigenous *Kuki* society practised the bride-price (Man khum) in marriage. This cultural practice once again augments respect and worth shown to a lady at the time of marriage. In some clans, the bride-price was more or less fixed with animals and traditional elements – shawls, lungis, necklaces, gongs, money, mithuns, etc. With marriage, a man becomes closely connected to the family of his wife. He pays the first bride-price at the earliest settlement of the marriage. Until the death of his wife, he continues to pay the bride-price in some form at different intervals. However rich or influential, he cannot exhaust payment of bride-price as long as his wife was alive. So, there is only one more chance to clear his due bride-price, that happens only after the death of his wife, before her burial rite begins. This practice signifies that a 'woman' is worth more than money and material wealth. A link exists between "life-style and death-style" (Davies, 2008, p. 2) where customs which were of importance continue even after death. The communitarian relationship and responsibility to each other that existed as the lifestyle continue even when one is dead.

While the dead body lies in the house, the husband (and his relatives, Bepa) are supposed to know the customary practice – to clear off the last payment of bride-price to the responsible family member of his dead wife. Then, the maternal uncles of the dead lady perform the *Ahkeng Khai,* a sign of forgiveness and farewell. After this customary regard, the *Thempu* and elders decide for digging of the grave and burial ritual begins. This is also a vivid sign of invoking maternal ancestral blessings for forgiveness, farewell and wish to meet again in *Mithi Kho*. We can see a chain of connectivity, that a child derives the name from his or her grandparent's name, seeks blessings in the form of *Lhalho*, *Akeng Khai* performed by maternal lineage, a woman's bride-price received by her paternal lineage. From birth till death, ancestor's roles were and are plenty in the indigenous *Kuki* society.

The *Thempu* remained as an intercessor for man and woman, and to perform death rituals without any discrimination. Today, the Catholic priest is a symbol of weak humanity "who offers sacrifices for his sins and the sins of the people" (Heb 5:3). In the Catholic tradition, a priest is present at marriage, birth, baptism, and accompanies the people till the rituals of the death. So, indigenous *Thempu* and Catholic priests are called upon to be faithful in their vocation and remain as intercessors for people in the cycle of life.

5.2.4. Indigenous Ecological Care

The *Thempu* constantly sought the mighty intervention of the omnipresent God who created the universe. In all rituals of indigenous *Thempu*, sense of respect was shown to animals sacrificed, trees fell, rivers or streams used, mountains cultivated, etc. These natural elements were considered sacred, possessing a spirit or soul created by the same creator who has created human beings. Ecology was respected and carefully used. Today, the sense of awe at God's creation is diminishing in the indigenous *Kuki* society.

Nature was the lone source for livelihood in the indigenous *Kuki* society. Their feasts, festivals, sickness, cure, success and failure were all associated with nature. Ignacimuthu (2010) scholarly pointed out that for tribals, "environment is not seen as a raw material for human consumption to be manipulated in whatever way people choose. Rather it is filled with spirit-presence and as such must be respected" (p. 45). Care for nature was ingrained in the minds of indigenous *Kuki* society as much as it was already found in the first book of the Bible "to till it and keep it" (Gen 2:15). After the flood, God made a covenant with Noah and said, "As for me I am establishing my covenant with you and your descendants, after you, and with every living creature that is with you, the birds, the domestic animals, and every animal of the earth with you, as many as came out of the ark" (Gen 8:9-10). The covenant God has established with every living creature is also a sign of respect to what he has created.

Everything in and around an indigenous *Kuki* was considered possessing a spirit. This belief made them consider natural elements as extensions of God. One could cut a tree for use but should not cut a tree just for its sake. Before cutting a tree, the indigenous *Kuki* ritual goes this way, "O tree, I need you to warm my house, I need you to support my roof. I cut you, not out of any sadistic nature but out of need." Every step taken for day-to-day survival was considered sacred. The *Thempu* would invoke God's blessing on occasions of *using a new stream, choosing a site for a new village, choosing a new house site, clearing forest for jhum cultivation, etc.* Indigenous practices of old teach us a shift from the anthropocentric and individualistic perception of the world (Hart, 2004) to the biblically-based vision of humanity unified with its habitat - the biotic and abiotic elements.

From the Yahwist account of creation, we read in Genesis 2:15 "The Lord God took the man and placed him in the garden of Eden to *till it* and *keep it*." This 'till it' and 'keep it' command was to produce, flourish and replicate itself as the years go by. Sacredness accorded to nature and all its content prompted the indigenous *Kuki* society to view nature as a potent manifestation of God. The belief that a sick person could recover from animal-sacrifice also has its foundation in the belief that all animals were sacred. Therefore, a sacred animal could redeem human life considered sacred in the eyes of God. They believed that the sacrifice of the sacred blood of the animal could redeem the sacred life of a human person. Above all, it was the *Thempu's* duty and the societal onus to *keep* human life.

Unfortunately, the present human tendency of capitalistic ownership of the garden (earth) is not the biblical vision of the Creator. The Psalmist sings, "The earth is the Lord's and all that is in it, the world, and those who live in it; for he has founded it on the seas, and established it on the rivers" (Ps 24:1-2). The earth belongs to God, we are mere creatures of His hands. Pope Francis laments about human's unlimited and selfish exploitation of ecology. In *Laudato Si* (2015), Francis refers to the earth, saying, "This sister now cries out to us because of the harm we have inflicted on her by our irresponsible use and abuse of the goods with which God has endowed her. We have come to see ourselves as her lords and masters, entitled to plunder her at will" (no. 2). Gonsalves (2015) supplements the stand of Pope Francis thus, "As members of Christ's Mystical Body, the Church, we must acknowledge our own individual sins and bear corporate responsibility for societal-structural sins and global-ecological-cosmic crises" (p. 213). The author further states that baptism is an entry "into a complex web of relationships with God-others-cosmos and strive to live life fully" (p. 216). This relationship gives us the unspoken responsibility to care, preserve and enhance. The beauty of creation is in nature and humans. On the extreme pole, ecological equilibrium is disturbed with the onslaught of globalization, trade and commerce. Selfishness is almost presumed as goodness and value.

The indigenous *Kuki* symbol of religion depicted in *Indoi/ Doibom* symbol, where best elements of nature were stuck together to represent *Pathen* was an obvious sign of respect for God's creation. The practice of seeking permission from spirits before use of new streams, a site for new village and forest for cultivation also symbolized respect shown to nature. Another clear sign, that of the common decision in the village under the leadership of *Haosa* administration to cultivate a particular area for a year was to avoid untoward exploitation of nature according to each individual's wish. Haokip (2006) points out the normal annual assembly of a *Kuki* village community held at the chief's residence called as the *Inpi* (Assembly) where common decisions for the following year was usually decided upon. This particular indigenous wisdom under the governance of *Haosa*, for common cultivation of a particular spot, has contributed to the economical use of land for survival. This allows nature to replicate itself with the passage of years and provides chances to help each other during cultivation. These indigenous rituals and practices sum up the belief that God or spirits were present everywhere in the human habitat.

When man and woman are "subjugated to anything or anyone, the whole evolution is reversed, the whole of creation is affected... When people enslave themselves to greed, lust, hatred, fear, anger and the like they are in sin; sin affects human beings, nature and the whole cosmos" (Mattam, 2015, p. 45). From the commerce lens, accumulation of wealth by destroying nature may be a value but from the Christian theological perspective, it is sin against nature, sin against the creator (God) and a new form of enslavement. It is an intentional surrender of self to wealth and appellation. Mattam (2015) firmly states, "The sacramentality of nature, the sacredness of the earth as a place where God reveals Himself calls forth from human beings much greater care of the Earth" (p. 46). The indigenous *Kuki* mode of considering nature as a sacred sanctuary where God and spirits dwelt is fading fast from the present generation of *Kukis*. On the contrary, several trucks are bought for logging, timber and wood sale. Nature is ultimately destroyed for the sake of money and affluence. The spirit of sharing one's wealth is fading away from the indigenous *Kuki* society.

5.3. Scope and Limitations of the Research

This research was conducted amongst the *Kuki* tribe of Manipur, with a limited number of participants, within two months (April-May 2018). The outcome of this study is based on primary data collection (semi-structured questionnaire, in-depth personal interviews). Therefore, these results are indicators of the people in the research area. As the literature review suggests, *Kukis,* dispersed in various states of India and different countries of the world live in different political, economic, social and religious situations. To arrive at a more holistic picture of the situation of the people, a larger project is needed at additional places where *Kukis* reside and indigenous *Thempu* tradition is or was in practice. Further research may notice deeper and elaborate qualitative treatment to indigenous *Thempu* tradition itself and excavate more themes of the tradition relevant for today's liturgical celebration in the context of pastoral ministry for Catholic priests and non-Catholic religious leaders. Further research would encourage thoughtful relevant contextual-embedded qualitative studies. Polyvocal work of this bend could mutually complement to the knowledge reservoir leading to an isomorphic outcome on *Thempu.*

One of the best ways to know about a culture is to enter as a learner into their social life to unearth their experiences. In many ways, indigenous practices of different cultures serve as treasure house to theologize for effective pastoral management. Research is one important means to arrive at scientific discovery for better pastoral administration and human contact. This study will enable the Catholic Church in Manipur to understand how traditional symbolism and rituals could be adapted into Catholic liturgy and further enrich it. Thus, this study could assist in creating variations in the liturgical worship that could be more appealing to those of the indigenous *Kuki* tribes. The uniqueness of knowledge gathered from various parts of Manipur resembles each other and gives specific details for further reflection. This diversity has contributed to the richness of the research proper.

5.4. Implications of the Research in Pastoral Ministry

The call to indigenous *Thempu* was voluntary, involving continuous learning, persistent association with *Thempus*, humility to learn and be amended. The *Thempu* represented a symbol of connectivity between the human world and the world of spirits. The biblical concept of a priest as an intercessor who knows the feelings of people and sympathizes with them has been spotted in the indigenous *Kukis* before Christianity came in. The *Thempu* offered gifts and sacrifices to spirits for the (presumed) faults of his people. He accepted the vocation to *Thempu*, not with pride but out of humility as called by God (Hebrews 5:1-4). Though there was no big remuneration, he accepted to be a *Thempu*.

The fundamental orientation to be a *Thempu* was to work for the welfare of others. The *Thempu* was a person who accompanied the members of the village from the moment of birth to tears of the tomb. This can be taken as spiritual, physical, psychological and social support he rendered to the people in their journey of life.

To nurture that 'service dimension' of indigenous *Kuki Thempu* of old will be one practical tool towards effective pastoral ministry. His assistance to the chief of the village and attention to the needs of the villagers was his personal contribution to the smooth functioning of the local self-government.

Christianity had its roots in Judeo-Hellenistic society but can all those cultural shades as found in the Bible be transplanted in indigenous *Kuki* society? As Pastors, situating oneself and the immediate environment are helpful ways to administer in one's pastoral ministry. Berkley (2004) writes, "People stress us! Pastors don't stress primarily because computers break down or earthquakes rattle the rafters. The most significant stressors for pastors spring from the conflicts, crises, and connivances of ordinary human beings" (p. 64). Menamparampil (2008) observed in a similar vein, stating, "The one who can give us many troubles can give us mighty help as well. A person of many abilities, who is capable of independent thought, is inclined to be assertive and vocal" (p. 27). The author continues to augment that "very often originality of thought, creativity, and special gifts seeking to express themselves, become the occasions for the difficulty in inter-personal relationships" (p. 27). This kind of conflict can arise when a pastor goes to ministry with rigid forms of administration and management learnt from books or taught in classrooms. Sometimes, even cultural ethos and indigenous practices of people could be conceived as a threat or hindrance. However, at a deeper reflection with open-mindedness, these so-called "threats or hindrances" can be occasions for creativity and maturity in life. As a scientific ethnographer, one should set out to learn from others than test one's preconceived principles.

Menamparampil succinctly pointed out, "Jesus had a firm grip on his audience and stirred wonder and admiration in his hearers, because, while his words had an immediate relevance, they addressed the central concerns of humanity" (2008, p. 138). In the pastoral ministry too, addressing the basic concerns of people like physical health, emotional wellbeing, culture and education can be ways for effective interaction with people. A pastor could use local images, myths, practices, idioms, similes, metaphors, proverbs and cultural practices to communicate the message of the gospel for relevant and effective pastoral ministry. Jesus stands out as example par excellence in his use of local practices to display his message: washing of feet as a sign of humility and service (Jn 13:1-17), the parable of the good shepherd (Jn 10:1-18), use of local bread and wine to indicate the sacrifice of his body and blood (Matt 26:20-30; Mk 14:17-26; Jn 13:21-30), the command to go and show themselves to the priests (Lk 17:14), etc. Respecting local ethos and consequently evolving new reflections for people was the pastoral plan of Jesus Christ.

Conclusion

Intense observation of the ancient practices of the indigenous *Kuki Thempu* can bring about appreciating culture and interpret Christianity in a fresh pastoral way without diluting the Bible. The researcher believes that indigenous *Thempu* tradition and Catholic priesthood can enhance each other by collaborating traditional and biblical practices. Revisiting one's cultural roots, relishing those rich cultural heritages of indigenous *Thempu*, and prudent integration with Catholic priesthood could make the liturgy more relevant to a contemporary audience who are modern but rooted in their erstwhile cultural heritage. Alertness and openness to change while embracing good practices of culture and religion will add beauty to Christianity and enliven pastoral ministry.

After research and reflection, the researcher begins to see that almost every ritual performed was a theologically oriented interaction for the performer, witnesses and attendees. Signs were gathered from elements of nature for healing and posterity. The question one can ask today is "Can the indigenous *Kukis* be still Christians without being too much influenced by western Christianity?" The rich indigenous heritage handed down through custom and culture can be interpreted with Christian values. Francis (2015) states, "Culture is more than what we have inherited from the past; it is also, and above all, a living, dynamic and participatory present reality, which cannot be excluded as we rethink the relationship between human beings and the environment" (Laudato Si, no. 143). Culture is an ongoing dynamism between humans and nature.

When Indigenous *Thempu* Tradition, Spirit of Forgiveness, Belief in a place for the Dead, Respect for Human Life, Spirit of Detachment, Respect for Women, Indigenous Ecological Care are acknowledged as cultural capital, then spiritual capital from the scripture and tradition can be authentically promoted for common good. This is like awakening the third eye to see the reality within with its possibilities – to concentrate on nature, others, and life to come. There is room to appreciate the patterns within cultural capital for mutual enhancement of Christianity and indigenous culture. Therefore, indigenous culture and biblical traditional assets can be considered as footprints of God on earth, signposts for the present generation.

General Conclusion

Knowing a cultural setting becomes a point of arrival with a departure note of journey. The sure mode to know people is to find them where they are, not where one expects them to be. For this, a pastor could use *local images, myths, practices, idioms, similes, metaphors, proverbs and cultural practices* as learning aids to bring gospel message for relevant and effective pastoral ministry. Openness to inculturation without diluting gospel values, upholding worthy cultural practices and equipping every pastor for ministerial responsibilities are desirable tools for theologizing today. The researcher tries to relate and convey sufficiently appreciative elements of indigenous *Kuki Thempu* tradition that could be of relevance and an asset to the present Catholic priesthood in particular and Christian leadership in general.

The indigenous *Kuki* belief in being healed from animal sacrifices gave optimism of redemption from 'offences' or 'sins' supposedly committed against spirits of nature. Jesus Christ, who has come to redeem humankind was received with a welcome gesture in the indigenous *Kuki* society. This calm welcome has its root in the already existent practice of indigenous *Thempu* who propitiates for humans with the blood sacrifice of animals. Restoration of life as found in the words of Jesus, "I came that they may have life, and have it abundantly" (Jn 10:10b) is a message appealing to an indigenous *Kuki* ear. Thus, Christianity has a stronghold in the indigenous *Kuki* society today.

There is a pressing need for cultural insertion into the Catholic priesthood for a meaningful celebration of sacraments with effective relevance for pastoral ministry. Taking into account the universal responsibility of being relevant in a local context, pastors can march forward with indigenous knowledge coupled with biblical truths. Collaboration, not only with people but their cultural ethos is also an important element for evangelization and meaningful expression of the gospel. Then, we can "make our contribution to the noble task of evangelization by developing a well-thought-out pastoral plan with the help of persons concerned and carrying it out effectively" (Manamparampil, 2008, p. 35).

Ardent observation of ancient practices of indigenous societies can bring about appreciating their culture to interpret Catholic priesthood in a new pastoral environment. Experiences of the past and present-day can absorb each other for a relevant pastoral ministry. Rather than having 'ready-made answers', asking 'Relevant Questions' of and for indigenous *Kuki* culture and Christianity could integrate traditional wisdom with biblical practices to blossom Christianity in context.

In the light of the research, certain proposals have been made for faithful preservation of indigenous *Kuki Thempu* wisdom while adapting to Catholic Christian culture. The indigenous culture of care for the earth, respect for life, health care and inclusive growth of the villagers can shed light and enhance the present socio-theological realms towards scientific debate and collaborative endeavours for humankind.

While Christianity is a blessing in many ways, it should be received with a pinch of salt as it has hampered indigenous blossoming of culture. The research has revealed that many indigenous *Kuki* traditions are fading with the arrival of Christianity and the latter's vehement condemnation of indigenous cultural practices was a reality. The research remains an attempt to give fresh implications to the erstwhile meaningful indigenous *Kuki Thempu* cultural practices for a harmonious integration with Christian tradition journeying towards an effective pastoral ministry.

References

Agu, A. (2009). *Responding to the Divine Call.* Mumbai: St Pauls.

Auer, J., & Ratzinger, J. (1988). *Eschatology: Death and Eternal Life.* Washington D.C.: The Catholic University of America Press.

Barbara, A, S., & Deryck, O, L. (2018). *Manipur State, India.* Retrieved from https://www.britannica.com/place/Manipur.

Barnes, M. H. (2000). *In the Presence of Mystery: An Introduction to the Story of Human Religiousness.* Connecticut: Twenty-Third Publications.

Bender, M. (2012). An Approach to Cultural Mapping in North-East India in Respect to Tribal Tales. *Asian Ethnology*, 71 (1), 148-150.

Berkley, J. D. (2004). *Leadership Handbook of Management and Administration.* Secunderabad: Om Books.

Bouyer, L. (1999). *The Invisible Father.* Edinburg: St. Bede's Publications.

Braaten, C. E., & Jenson, W. (2002). *The Last Things: Biblical and Theological Perspectives on Eschatology.* UK: WM. B. Eerdmans Publishing Co.

CBCI. (2007). Vision, Mission and Goals. *Catholic Bishops Conference of India.* Retreived from https://www.cbci.in/AICEP-2007-Chapter2.aspx.

Changsan, D. M. (1992). Basic Beliefs of the Traditional Kuki Religion. *Journal of Dharma: Dharmaram Journal of Religions and Philosophies, 17,* 98-109. Retrieved from www.dharmaramjournals.in/.../Basic%20Beliefs%20of%20 the%20Traditional%20Kuk...

Chongloi, H. (2008). *Indoi: A Study of Primal Kuki Religious Symbolism in the Hermeneutical Framework of Mircea Eliade.* Delhi: ISPCK.

Chongloi, L. (2013). Culture Change among the Kukis: A Case Study of Chalva Village in Manipur. *Journal of North East India Studies 3 (1), 18-30.* Retrieved from https://works.bepress.com/jneis/25/.

Chryssides, G. (2014). Insider and outsider. In Chryssides. G., & Geaves, R. (Eds.), *The Study of Religion: An Introduction to Key Ideas and Methods* (pp. 67-88). London: Bloomsbury.

Congregation for the Doctrine of the Faith, (1987). *Donum Vitae: The Instruction on Respect for Human Life in its Origin and on the Dignity of Procreation.* Retrieved from www.vatican.va/.../rc_con_cfaith_doc_19870222_respect-for-human-life_en.html.

Davies, D. J. (2008). *The Theology of Death.* New York: T&T Clark.

Dunfee. J. M. (2009). *Priest: Alter Christus. Our Sunday Visitor.* 15 Dec 2009 Retrieved from https://www.osv.com/OSVNewsweekly/Story/TabId/.../Priest-Alter-Christus.aspx.

Dupius, J., & Neuner, J. (2011). *The Christian Faith.* Bangalore: Theological Publications in India.

Francis. (2014). *To All Consecrated People: Apostolic letter on the Occasion of the Year of Consecrated Life.* Retrieved from www.marleygrangeparish.ie/wp-content/uploads/.../Year-of-Consecrated-Life2.pdf

Francis. (2018). *Gaudete Et Exsultate: Apostolic Exhortation on the Call to Holiness in Today's World.* Retrieved from w2.vatican.va/.../papa-francesco_esortazione-ap_20180319_gaudete-et-exsultate.htm.

F. S., Lalitha. (2018). Sinning Against Ourselves and God. In Pandikattu. K., & Vadappuram. J. M., (Eds.), *Francis Effect: Fifty-One Articles on Pope Francis' Insights* (pp. 87-89). Pune: Jnanam Publications.

Gangte, P. M. (2010). *Evolution of Kuki Chieftainship through Customary Laws – Its Modern Conceptuality.* Retrieved from http://kukiforum.com/2010/12/evolution-of-kuki-chieftainship-through-customary-laws-its-modern-conce.

Garvey, J. (2005). *Death and the Rest of Our Life.* UK: WM. B. Eerdmans Publishing Co.

Gonsalves, F. (2015). *Feet Rooted, Hearts Radiant, Minds Raised, Living Sacraments in India.* Anand: Gujarat Sahitya Prakash.

Greenberg, Y. K. (2018). *The Body in Religion: Cross-Cultural Perspectives.* London: Bloomsbury.

Haokip, D. S. (2006). *A Study on the Traditional Religion of the Kukis before the Advent of Christianity.* (Unpublished: Thesis Submitted to Manipur University in Partial Fulfilment for the Award of the Degree of Doctor of Philosophy in History. Registration No. 108 of 1999). *Retrieved from shodhganga.inflibnet.ac.in/handle/10603/103667.*

Haokip, H. (n.d.) *Myth: A Source for Doing Tribal Theology with Special Reference to the Kuki Tribes of Manipur.* Unpublished bachelor of divinity thesis. Senate of Serampore College, Serampore.

Haokip, J. (2015). *Colonisation, Identity and Search for Peace.* Pune: Print Art Enterprises.

Haokip, L. (2000). *Thempuho Thu.* Churachandpur: Maranatha Printers.

Haokip, P. (1979). *Kuki Culture and the Christian Message: Theologizing in the Context of Kuki Culture.* Unpublished master's thesis, Jnana-Deepa Vidyapeeth, Institute of Philosophy and Religion, Pune.

Haokip, P. (2017). Traditional Material Culture of the Kukis of Manipur with Special Reference to their Marriage System and Practices. *International Journal of Innovative Research and Advanced Studies (IJIRAS), 4 (5),* 273-277. Retrieved from www.ijiras.com/2017/Vol_4-Issue_5/paper_57.pdf.

Haokip. P. S. (2006). *The Culture and Tradition of the Kuki People.* Retrieved from kukiforum.com/2006/01/the-culture-and-tradition-of-the-kuki-people/

Haokip, P. S. (2008). *Zale'n-Gam: The Kuki Nation.* India: Saurabh Printers.

Haokip, N., & Lunminthang, M. eds. (2011). *Kuki Society: Past, Present, Future.* Delhi: Maxford Books.

Haring, B. (1976). *The Sacraments in a Secular Age.* England: St. Paul Publications.

Hoffman, D., & Cole, B., (2001). *Consecrated Life.* Mumbai: St. Pauls.

Ignacimuthu S. S. J. (2010). *Environmental Spirituality.* Mumbai: St. Paul's.

Israel, M. (1976). *Precarious Living.* London and New York: Continuum.

John Paul II. (1981). *Familiaris Consortio: Apostolic Exhortation to the Episcopate, to the Clergy and to the Faithful of the whole Catholic Church on the Role of the Christian Family in the Modern World.* Retrieved from w2.vatican.va/content/john...ii/.../hf_jp-ii_exh_19811122_familiaris-consortio.html.

John Paul II. (1987). *Donum Vitae: Instruction on Respect for Human Life in its Origin and on the Dignity of Procreation.* Retrieved from www.vatican.va/.../rc_con_cfaith_doc_19870222_respect-for-human-life_en.html.

John Paul II. (1992). *Patores Dabo Vobis: Post-Synodal Apostolic Exhortation to the Bishops, Clergy and Faithful on the Formation of Priests in the Circumstances of the Present Day.* Retrieved from w2.vatican.va/content/john...ii/.../hf_jp-ii_exh_25031992_pastores-dabo-vobis.html.

John Paul II. (1995). *Evangelium Vitae: To the Bishops, Priests and Deacons, Men and Women Religious, Lay Faithful and all People of Good Will on the Value and Inviolability of Human Life.* Retrieved from w2.vatican.va/content/john-paul-ii/.../hf_jp-ii_enc_25031995_evangelium-vitae.html.

John Paul II. (1996). *Vita Consecreta: Post-Synodal Apostolic Exhortation to the Bishops and Clergy, Religious Orders and Congregations, Societies of Apostolic Life, Secular Institutes and all the Faithful on the Consecrated Life and its Mission in the Church and in the World.* Retrieved from w2.vatican.va/content/john-paul-ii/.../hf_jp-ii_exh_25031996_vita-consecrata.html.

Joseph, U. V. (2017). Family-Oriented Religious Literature: Focus on Vernacular Languages. *Oriens Journal for Contextual Theology,* VIII, 127-141.

Keenan, J. (2005). *Suffering, the Body and Christianity. Health Progress. May – June,* 53-59.

Kelly, D. F. (2004). *Contemporary Catholic Health Care Ethics.* Washington: Georgetown University Press.

Kipgen, N. (2012). *Kuki Identity, Land-Use, Authority, and Ethnic Nationalism in Manipur.* Unpublished doctoral thesis. Indian Institute of Technology. Delhi. Retrieved from https://www.isa-sociology.org › ... › Dissertation Abstracts › List of abstracts.

Kipgen, N. (2012). *Democratization of Kuki Tribal Polity in Contemporary Manipur.* Retrieved from http://hdl.handle.net/2080/1772.

Koireng, A. S., & Gangte, P. M. (2010). *Understanding Kuki since Primordial Times.* New Delhi: Maxford Books.

Maloney, G. (2007). *Communion of Saints.* Bangalore: I.J.A. Publications & Catholic Literature Bureau.

Mattam, J. (2015). *The Religious Life: Within a Christian Vision of Reality.* India: Gujarat Sahitya Prakash.

Macquarrie, J. (1998). *A Guide to the Sacraments.* New York: Continuum.

Menamparampil, T. (2008). *Never Grow Tired.* Mumbai: Pauline Publications.

Paul VI. (1963). *Sacrosanctum Concilium: Constitution on the Sacred Liturgy.* Retrieved from www.vatican.va/.../hist.../vat-ii_const_19631204_sacrosanctum-concilium_en.html.

Paul VI. (1964). *Lumen Gentium: Dogmatic Constitution on the Church.* Retrieved from www.vatican.va/archive/hist.../ii.../vat-ii_const_19641121_lumen-gentium_en.html.

Paul VI. (1965). *Gaudium Et Spes: Pastoral Constitution on the Church in the Modern World.* Retrieved from www.vatican.va/archive/hist.../ii.../vat-ii_const_19651207_gaudium-et-spes_en.html.

Paul VI. (1965). *Optatam Totius: Decree on Priestly Training.* Retrieved from www.vatican.va/archive/hist.../ii.../vat-ii_decree_19651028_optatam-totius_en.html.

Paul VI. (1965). *Presbyterorum Ordinis: Decree on the Ministry and Life of Priests.* Retrieved from www.vatican.va/archive/.../vat-ii_decree_19651207_presbyterorum-ordinis_en.html.

Paul VI. (1968). *Humanae Vitae: To His Venerable Brothers, the Patriarchs, Archbishops, Bishops and other Local Ordinaries in Peace and Communion with the Apostolic See, to the Clergy and Faithful of the whole Catholic World, and to all Men of Good Will, on the Regulation of Birth.* Retrieved from https://w2.vatican.va/content/paul-vi/.../hf_p-vi_enc_25071968_humanae-vitae.html.

Pius XII. (1984). *Mystici Corporis Christi: Encyclical on the Mystical Body of Christ, to our Venerable Brethren, Patriarchs, Primates, Archbishops, Bishops, and other*

Local Ordinaries enjoying Peace and Communion with the Apostolic See. Retrieved from w2.vatican.va/content/pius.../hf_p-xii_enc_29061943_mystici-corporis-christi.html.

Podimattam, F. M. (2008). *The Priest: 21st Century Perspectives.* Delhi: Media House.

Ponnore, J. (2016). *Spirituality of the Diocesan Priest.* Raipur: United Printers.

Pyysiäinen, I. (2004). *Magic, Miracles, and Religion.* Oxford: Altamira Press.

Raatan. T. (2006). *History, Religion and Culture of Northeast.* Delhi: Isha Books.

Reeves, S., Kuper, A., & Hodges, B., D. (2008). *Qualitative Research Methodologies: Ethnography.* Retrieved from https://doi.org/10.1136/bmj.a1020.

Rossetti, S. (2004). *The Joy of Priesthood.* Indiana: Ave Maria Press.

Sangasubana, N. (2011). How to Conduct Ethnographic Research. *The Qualitative Report, 567-573.* Retrieved from http://nsuworks.nova.edu/tqr/vol16/iss2/14

Schmidt-Leukel, P. (2017). *God Beyond Boundaries: A Christian and Pluralist Theology of Religions,* New York: Waxmann.

Serrao, C. (2010). *Discernment of Religious Vocation: Formation towards Transformation.* Bangalore: Dhyanavana Publications.

Shaw, W. (1929). *Notes on the Thadou Kukis. Edited with Introduction, Notes, Appendices, Illustrations and Index, by J. H. Hutton,* Calcutta: Asiatic Society of Bengal.

Sherry, P. (1984). *Spirit, Saints, Immortality.* Albany: State University of New York Press.

Warrington, K. (2006). A Spirit Theology of Suffering. In Hunter, H. D., & Robeck, C. M. JR. (Eds.), *The Suffering Body: Responding to the Persecution of Christians* (pp. 24-36). Great Britain: Paternoster Press.

Whitehead, E. A., & Whitehead, J. D. (1981). *Method in Ministry: Theological Reflection and Christian Ministry,* New York: The Seabury Press.

Appendix A

Questionnaire (English)

1. Can you describe people's or your understanding of *Thempu*?
2. What were the areas in which the *Thempu* helped people of the village?
3. Can you tell me something about the spirit world?
4. How did the *Thempu* appease spirits?
   a. What beliefs do the *Thempu* have about spirits?
   b. What were the rituals *Thempu* performed?
5. What roles did the *Thempu* play during ceremonies?
   a. What were the things *Thempu* used during rituals?
   b. What were the types of animals *Thempu* sacrificed?
   c. What else?
6. What training was required to become a *Thempu*?
7. What things were given to *Thempu* as remuneration?
8. What are the similarities and differences between *Thempu* and Catholic priest?
9. What is the relevance of *Thempu* today?

Appendix B

Questionnaire (Thadou-Kuki)

1. *Thempu chungchanghi mipite hetdan le nangma hetdan neiseipih theidem?*
2. *Thempu in khosungmite chu hoilai mun muna chu anakithopi ji em?*
3. *Thilha (lhagao) te hinkho chungchang neiseipih thei dem?*
4. *Thempu chun iti thilhate chu ana joldam ji em?*
    a. *Thempute'n thilhate chungchanga ngaidan ipi anei uvem?*
    b. *Thempu in mipite dia ipi kithoina kin ananei ji uvem?*
5. *Thempu in khosung vengsung kin aum tengle amopohna ipipi ham?*
    a. *Thempu in kithoina kin tengle ipi thil thil amanchah ji em?*
    b. *Thempu in kithoina kin tengle ipi sa sa anamanchah ji em?*
6. *Thempu hinadinga ipi themjil ngai ji em?*
7. *Thempu chun akin achai tengle khomite'n ipithil anapeh ji uvem?*
8. *Kuki Thempu le Catholic thempu akibahna le akikhel na neihil thei dem?*
9. *Tulai a Thempu kitihohin kimanchahna anei nalai hinam?*

Appendix C

Permission for Research

Most Rev. Dominic Lumon, D.D.
ARCHBISHOP OF IMPHAL

ARCHBISHOP'S HOUSE
P.B. No. 35, IMPHAL - 795 001
MANIPUR, INDIA

Phone : 0385 - 2427620 (P), 2421292 (H) 09436023449 (Mob.) Fax : 0385 - 2427628 e-mail : lumondominic@gmail.com

<u>TO WHOM IT MAY CONCERN</u>

12/03/2018

This is to certify that Fr. Paul Lelen Haokip, a priest of the Archdiocese of Imphal, Manipur, who is currently pursuing Master's Degree in Pastoral Management (MPM) at Jnana – Deepa Vidyapeeth, Pune, Maharashtra, India, has been granted permission to conduct a research study on "***UNDERSTANDING OF THEMPU AND CATHOLIC PRIESTHOOD: AN ETHNOGRAPHIC STUDY***" within the Archdiocese of Imphal, Manipur, India.

Kindly extend him whatever help you can in his research so that he can successfully and fruitfully complete his work.

+ Dominic Lumon D.D.,
Archbishop of Imphal,
Manipur, India